THE Third
Chimpanzee

FOR YOUNG PEOPLE

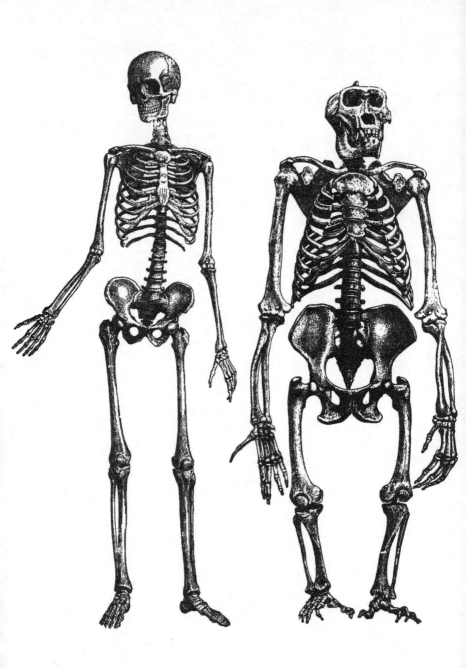

THE Third Chimpanzee

FOR YOUNG PEOPLE

ON THE EVOLUTION AND FUTURE
OF THE HUMAN ANIMAL

JARED
DIAMOND

ADAPTED BY REBECCA STEFOFF

SEVEN STORIES PRESS
Triangle Square books for young readers

New York • Oakland

A SEVEN STORIES PRESS FIRST EDITION

Copyright © 2014 by Jared Diamond
For permissions information see page 369.

SEVEN STORIES PRESS
140 Watts Street
New York, NY 10013
www.sevenstories.com

College professors may order examination copies of Seven Stories Press titles for free. To order, visit www.sevenstories.com/textbook or send a fax on school letterhead to (212) 226-1411.

A teaching guide and lesson plan for *The Third Chimpanzee for Young People*, as well as other select titles within the Young People's series from Triangle Square / Seven Stories Press, is available for free download at www.sevenstories.com.

Book design by Pollen/Stewart Cauley, New York

Library of Congress Cataloging-in-Publication Data
Stefoff, Rebecca, 1951-
  Third chimpanzee for young people / by Jared Diamond ; adapted by Rebecca Stefoff. -- Seven Stories Press first edition.
    pages cm
  Adapted from Jared M. Diamond's The third chimpanzee.
  Includes index.
  ISBN 978-1-60980-522-7
  1. Human evolution--Juvenile literature. 2. Social evolution--Juvenile literature. 3. Nature--Effect of human beings on--Juvenile literature. I. Diamond, Jared M. II. Diamond, Jared M. Third chimpanzee. III. Title.
  GN281.S785 2014
  573.2--dc23

                                        2013040205

Printed in the United States

9 8 7 6 5 4 3 2 1

Contents

Introduction

WHAT MAKES US HUMAN?

HUMANS ARE DIFFERENT FROM ALL ANIMALS.
At the same time, humans *are* animals—a species
of big mammal. This contradiction is our most
fascinating feature. We still have a hard time
understanding what it means and how it came to be.

On one hand, between us and all other
species lies a gulf that leads us to call them
"animals" and to see them as separate from us.
We think that centipedes, chimpanzees, and
clams share some animal features that we don't
have, or that we have human features that they
don't share. Those human features include
communicating through language, enjoying
art, making complex tools, wearing clothes, and
darker traits such as killing mass numbers of
our own and other species.

On the other hand, we have the same body
parts, molecules, and genes as other animals. It's
even clear what type of animal we are. As long
ago as the eighteenth century, scientists who

studied anatomy (the structure of the body) saw that humans are very similar to chimpanzees, animals that live in Africa. We recognize two species of chimpanzees: the common chimp and the bonobo, sometimes called the pygmy chimp. A scientist from outer space would immediately classify humans as a third species of chimpanzee. Scientists right here on Earth know that we share more than 98 percent of our genetic makeup with the other two chimps.

The difference between our genes and chimps' genes is small. Yet that small difference must have been responsible for the things that make humans unique. And all those changes happened fairly recently in our genetic history. Somehow, within a few tens of thousands of years, we started to show the features that make humans unique and fragile. This book takes a close look at how and why we developed those features, both good and bad—from language, art, and our life cycle to our ability to destroy our own and other species.

How This Book Came to Be

My own interests and background shaped this book. As a child, I wanted to be a doctor. By my last year in college, that goal had gently changed, and I wanted to become a medical researcher. I trained in physiology, which is the study of how living systems function, from cells to animals. Afterward I went on to teach and do research at the University of California Medical School in Los Angeles.

But I had other interests as well. Birdwatching had attracted me since the age of seven, and I had also been lucky to attend a school that let me plunge into languages and history. I did not like the idea of spending the rest of my life on physiology alone. Then I had the chance to spend a summer in the highlands of New Guinea, a large tropical island north of Australia. The purpose of the trip was to measure how successfully birds were nesting. That project collapsed when I was unable to locate even a single bird's nest in the jungle, but the trip fed my thirst for adventure and birdwatching in one of the wildest remaining parts of the world.

After that first trip to New Guinea, I developed a second career, focused on birds, evolution, and biogeography. I've returned to New Guinea and the neighboring Pacific islands many times to pursue my bird research. As I saw human activity destroying the forests and birds I loved, I became involved in conservation, helping governments design national parks to protect ecosystems and plant and animal species.

Finally, it was hard to study the evolution and extinction of birds without wanting to understand the evolution and possible extinction of the most interesting species of all, the species that includes you, me, and everyone on Earth—*Homo sapiens*, the modern human. This book was the result. It begins with a look at our origins several million years ago. It ends with some thoughts about our future, and about ways we can learn from our past.

Building a Big Picture
The story of how we became human spans millions of years, and it pulls together information and ideas from many branches of science. In writing this book, I drew on my own experiences and the sciences I have studied, and also on the work of many scientists in other fields, from archaeology to

zoology. Pieces of the story come from fields as different as paleopathology, the study of ancient diseases, and paleobotany, the science of fossil plants.

As you've seen, my background started with anatomy and physiology, then moved on to the study of birds, especially their ecology—that is, the ways bird interact with other species around them and with their environment. As a biogeographer, I'm interested in the relationships between geography and living things. Biogeographers ask questions such as: Why are some species spread out across almost the entire world, while others live only in a single tree? As you'll see in this book, biogeography has played a big role in the history of our species.

I am also an evolutionary biologist. This means that I look at animals and plants in terms of evolution, the process of change in life on Earth over time, as new species develop and old ones become extinct. (In chapter 4, you'll read about how this happens.) In this book, I use the framework of evolutionary biology to examine human features and behavior.

Seeing Ourselves in a New Way

From a scientist's point of view, things often look different from the way they look in everyday life. Take the question of how people are attracted to each other. What do you find attractive in another person? There are as many answers to that question as there are individuals in the world.

But to an evolutionary biologist, the question takes on another dimension. Because we see the human species as part of the natural world, we assume that people are shaped by the same forces that shape other species. By looking for patterns in the way birds and mice and apes choose their mates, as I do in chapter 3, we expect to learn something about our own behavior.

In evolutionary terms, successful features and behaviors let parents produce the greatest number of children, who will eventually produce children of their own, passing the parents' genes on to new generations. This doesn't mean that evolutionary biology is the complete explanation, or the only explanation, for everything people do. It does mean that seeing ourselves as part of the evolutionary history of life enlarges our knowledge.

Looking at our own species in the same way we look at others can bring new understanding of human behavior that may seem confusing or mysterious, or make us uncomfortable. It is a way of knowing ourselves better—and the quest for self-knowledge is a very human characteristic.

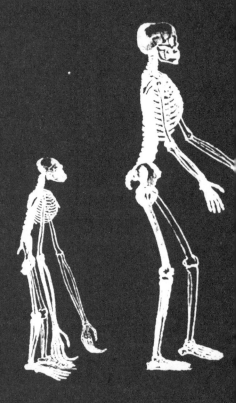

(*Left to right*:
Gibbon, Human,
Chimpanzee,
Gorilla,
Orangutan.)
Five members of
the primate family:
Homo sapiens and
four kinds of apes.
The similar anatomy
of human and ape
skeletons had been
recognized for centu-
ries, but DNA stud-
ies confirmed that
chimpanzees are our
closest relatives, and
we are theirs.

PART ONE

JUST ANOTHER
BIG MAMMAL

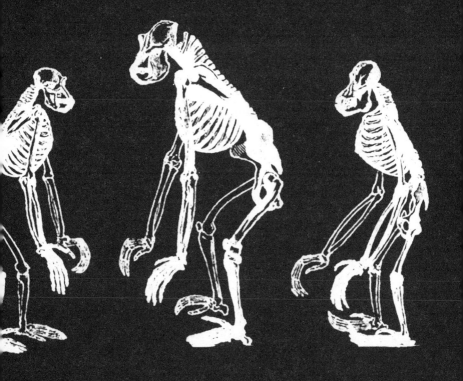

WHEN, WHY, AND HOW DID WE STOP BEING JUST another species of big mammal? Clues come from three types of evidence, all explored in the next two chapters. Fossil bones and preserved tools are traditional evidence from archaeology, the study of the past through physical remains. A newer kind of evidence comes from the science of molecular biology, which examines our genetic heritage and traces our descent from an apelike ancestor.

One basic question concerns the differences between us and chimpanzees. Just looking at humans and chimps and counting visible differences doesn't help, because many genetic changes have effects that can't be seen, while other changes have very obvious effects. A Great Dane and a Chihuahua look much more different from each other than a chimp and a human being do. Yet all dogs belong to the same species, but chimps and humans are different species.

So how can we tell our genetic distance from chimps? The problem has been solved by molecular biologists. They have discovered that the gene difference between us and chimps is greater than the difference between any two living human populations or any two breeds of dogs. But the gene difference between us and chimps is small compared with differences between many other pairs of related species. This means that only a small change in the chimpanzee genes led to enormous changes in humans' behavior.

Next we'll consider what we can learn from the bones and tools left by creatures along the way between our apelike ancestor and modern humans. Fossil bones show the switch from our walking on all fours to walking upright, and our increase in brain size. Our large brain was surely necessary for the development of human language and inventiveness. In fact, we might expect the fossil record to show our tools getting better as our brains got bigger. But the greatest surprise and puzzle of human evolution is that stone tools remained very crude for hundreds of thousands of years after our brains had expanded almost to their present size.

Sixty thousand years ago, Neanderthals had brains even larger than those of modern humans, yet their tools show no signs of inventiveness or art. Neanderthals were still just another species of big mammal. Even for tens of thousands of years after some other human populations had evolved skeletons like those of modern people, their tools remained as boring as Neanderthals' tools.

Within the small percentage of difference between our genes and chimpanzee genes, there must have been an even smaller percentage that was not involved in the shapes of our bones but that gave us the human traits of inventiveness, artistic creativity, and the use of complex tools. In Europe, at least, those traits appeared suddenly at the time Neanderthals were replaced by the early modern humans known as Cro-Magnons. That's when we finally stopped being just another species of big mammal. At the end of part 1, I'll talk about what triggered our steep rise to human status.

CHAPTER I
A TALE OF THREE CHIMPS

THE NEXT TIME YOU VISIT A ZOO, WALK PAST THE ape cages. Imagine that the apes had lost most of their hair and that next to them was a cage holding some unfortunate people who had lost their clothes and couldn't speak but were normal in every other way. Now try guessing how different the apes' genes are from the humans' genes. Would you guess that a chimpanzee shares 10 percent, 50 percent, or 99 percent of its genetic makeup with humans?

In recent decades, science has answered that question. Even though many other questions remain unanswered, we now know more about our origins than ever before. Every human society has felt a deep need to make sense of its origins, and has met that need with its own story of creation. The creation story of our time is the tale of three chimps.

Three Questions

For centuries it's been clear roughly where we fit into the animal kingdom. We are mammals, part of the group of animals that have hair and nurse their young. Among mammals, we are primates, the group of mammals that includes monkeys and apes. We share primate features that most non-primates do not have, including flat fingernails and toenails (rather than claws), hands for gripping, and thumbs that can move in the opposite direction from our fingers.

Within the primates, we are more similar to apes (gorillas, chimpanzees, orangutans, and gibbons) than to monkeys. For one thing, monkeys have tails, but apes and humans do not. Gibbons stand out from the other apes because they are small and have very long arms. Gorillas, chimpanzees, orangutans, and humans are more closely related to one another than any of them is to gibbons.

Going further into our primate relationships proved difficult for scientists. It led to an intense debate centered on three questions:

* **What is the detailed family tree of relationships among humans, the living ape species, and the extinct ape species that were our ancestors? If**

we knew the answer to this question, we would know which living ape is our closest relative.

* When did we and our closest living relative last share the same ancestor? This would tell us how long ago the human line branched off the family tree.

* How much of our genetic makeup do we share with our closest living relative? This would tell us what percentage of our genes is uniquely human.

Fossil evidence might answer the first two questions, except for one unfortunate fact. Almost no ape fossils have been found for the crucial period between five and fourteen million years ago in Africa. Instead, the answers to the questions came from an unexpected source: a project to sort out relationships among bird species.

A Clue from the Bird World
In the 1960s, molecular biologists began to realize that the chemicals that make up plants and animals might provide "clocks" to measure the genetic distances between species, and to tell how long ago those species separated from each other on the evolutionary tree. Take lions and tigers, for example.

Suppose we knew from fossils that lions and tigers separated five million years ago. Suppose that a certain molecule in lions was 1 percent different from the same molecule in tigers. That would mean that 1 percent of genetic difference equaled five million years of separate evolution. Then, if scientists wanted to compare two living species but had no fossils to show those species' evolutionary history, they could look at that same molecule in both species. If the difference between the two molecules was 3 percent, they would know that the species separated from their shared ancestor about fifteen million years ago—that is, three times five million.

In the 1970s, two scientists named Charles Sibley and Jon Ahlquist used the idea of a molecular clock based on changes in DNA to study the evolutionary relationships of about 1,700 bird species, nearly a fifth of all living birds. A decade later, they used the same techniques to study primate evolution. For this project they examined the DNA of humans and all our closest relatives: common chimpanzees, bonobos (or pygmy chimpanzees), gorillas, orangutans, two species of gibbons, and seven species of monkeys. Their results gave us a new understanding of the primate family tree.

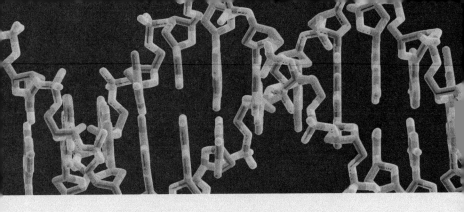

A CLOCK MADE OF DNA

THE MOLECULAR CLOCK WORKS THIS WAY:
Suppose some type of molecule existed in all
species, but had a unique structure in each
species. Suppose that structure changed
slowly over millions of years because of genetic
mutations, and suppose the rate of change was
the same for all species.

Two species that descended from the same
ancestor would start off with identical forms
of the molecule, inherited from their ancestor.
Over time, though, mutations would occur
independently in each line of descent. These
mutations would change the structure of that
molecule in each of the two species. We could
measure the present difference in the molecule's
structure between the two. Then, if we knew how
many structural changes occurred, on average,
every million years, the present difference

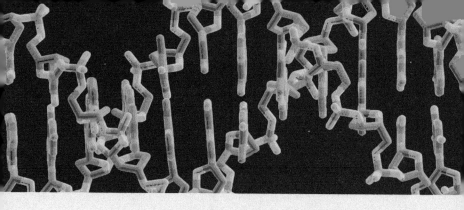

between the two species would serve as a "clock," telling us how much time had passed since the two species shared a common ancestor.

By around 1970, molecular biologists had found that the best "clock" molecule is deoxyribonucleic acid, or DNA. It occurs in all living things but is unique to each species. DNA is made up of two long chains of molecules. Each chain is made up of four types of small molecules. The sequence, or order, of those small molecules carries all the genetic information that is passed from parents to offspring.

To measure changes in DNA structure, scientists use a method called DNA hybridization. They mix the DNA from two species, then measure the melting point of this mixed, or hybrid, DNA. The next step is to compare the melting point of the hybrid DNA with the melting point of pure DNA from a single species. A difference of about

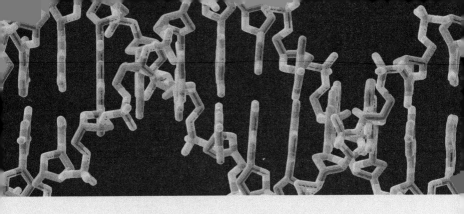

one degree centigrade means that the two species differ by about 1 percent of their DNA.

The final stage is to calibrate, or set, the DNA clock. This means linking DNA change to the passage of time. We might know that two species' DNA differs by 1 percent, but until we know how DNA changes over time, we can't know how long the two species have been evolving separately. To calibrate the DNA clock, scientists use species whose evolutionary history is known from fossils that can be accurately dated. In the case of birds, studies of both fossils and DNA from living bird species reveal that one gene in DNA (the gene called cytochrome b) appears to change by 1 percent every one million years. Using this information, scientists can measure the differences in cytochrome b in any two living bird species and tell how long ago those species separated from the ancestor they shared.

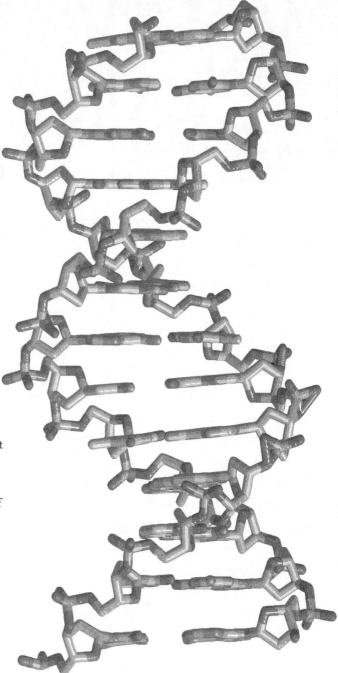

A key to understanding connections among living things lies in DNA, the genetic material within our cells. It is made up of two long strands of molecules linked by shorter pairs of molecules, like a ladder with many rungs that has been twisted into a spiral—a shape known as a double helix.

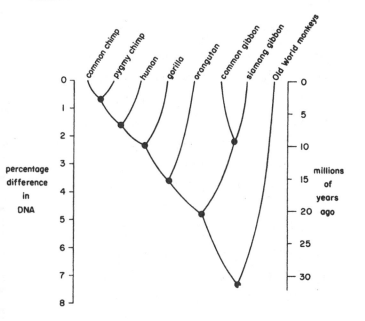

FIGURE I

A family tree of evolutionary relationships among primates, including humans. Black dots represent the last time two groups shared
the same ancestor. The scale on the right measures time and the
scale on the left measures differences in the DNA of living species.
Start with the dot on the bottom right—that's the point, more than
30 million years ago, when apes separated from the monkeys of
Eurasia and Africa. The monkeys kept evolving right up to the present. As the apes evolved, gibbons split off into their own line about
20 million years ago. The black dot marking that split is at 5 percent
on the DNA scale, because gibbons differ in 5 percent of their DNA
from other apes and humans. The second black dot from the left
shows humans and chimpanzees splitting about 7 million years ago,
with a difference of less than 2 percent in the DNA of humans and
chimpanzees today.

The Primate Family Tree

When scientists studied the molecular clock in primate DNA, they found that the biggest genetic difference is between monkeys on one hand and apes and humans on the other. This came as no surprise. Ever since apes became known to science, everybody has agreed that humans and apes are more closely related to each other than either of them is to monkeys. The molecular clock showed that monkeys differ from humans and apes in 7 percent of their DNA structure.

The clock also confirmed that gibbons are the most distinct apes. They differ from the other apes and humans in 5 percent of their DNA structure. Orangutans differ in 3.6 percent from gorillas, chimpanzees, and humans. These findings show that gibbons and orangutans separated from the rest of the ape family long ago. Today, gibbons and orangutans are found only in Southeast Asia. In contrast, gorillas and chimpanzees are found only in Africa, which was also the home of the earliest humans. Among apes, the most closely related living species are the two types of chimpanzees, common chimps and bonobos. Their DNA is 99.3 percent identical.

What about humans? We differ from gorillas in about 2.3 percent of our DNA, and from chimps of both species by about 1.6 percent. This means that we share 98.4 percent of our DNA with chimpanzees, our closest living relatives. Put another way, the chimpanzee's closest relative is not the gorilla—it is the human.

Calibrated for primate species, the DNA clock shows that gorillas separated from the line leading to chimps and humans about ten million years ago. Ancestral humans separated from chimps about seven million years ago. In other words, humans have been evolving on their own for something like seven million years.

The genetic distance separating us from chimps is less than the distance between two species of gibbons (2.2 percent). In an example from the bird world, the red-eyed vireo and white-eyed vireo are species of songbirds. Both belong to the same genus, or cluster of closely related species. But they differ in 2.9 percent of their DNA—much more than the difference between us and chimps. In terms of genetic distance, humans, common chimps, and bonobos should be grouped in the same genus. Looked at this way, humans are a third species of chimpanzee.

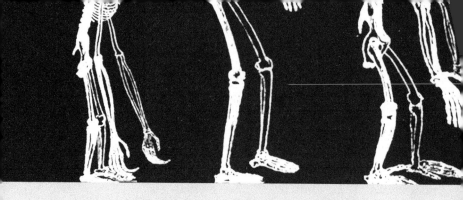

HOW SHOULD WE TREAT APES?

NOW THAT WE KNOW HOW SMALL A GENETIC distance separates us from chimps, our ideas about the places of humans and apes may change over time. One area that might change is the way we treat apes. Ethical issues—that is, questions of what is right and wrong—are involved.

It's considered acceptable to exhibit caged apes in zoos, but it's not acceptable to do the same thing with humans. Yet if it were not for the interest in apes that many people gain by visiting zoos, the public might contribute much less money to protect apes in the wild. How will we balance our desire to collect chimpanzees and other apes in zoos with our knowledge that we are so closely related to chimps?

Medical experimentation on chimpanzees is a controversial subject. It is unethical, or wrong, to perform experiments on humans without their knowledge and consent. Why is it okay to perform such experiments on chimps? If we

say it is because chimps are animals, then we are saying they are no different from insects and bacteria in terms of what we can do with them, because insects and bacteria are also animals. But if we consider intelligence, social organization, and the ability to feel pain, it becomes hard to draw an all-or-nothing line between all humans and all animals. Instead, different ethical rules should apply to research on different species. If there is any animal species now used in medical research for which we could argue that all experimentation should stop, that species is surely the chimpanzee.

Making matters worse, chimps used for research are often caged under cruel conditions. The first research chimp that I saw had been injected with a slow-acting deadly virus. It was being kept alone for several years, in a small indoor cage, with nothing to play with, until it died. And the capture of wild chimps for research usually means that several wild

chimps are killed to capture one, which is often a youngster being carried by its mother.

Yet the very reason medical researchers use chimps is that they are so genetically similar to us. Experiments on apes are a far better way to improve medical treatments than experiments on any other animals. Researchers are now studying certain diseases in captive chimps. How would we explain to parents whose children are at risk of dying from those diseases that their children are less important than chimps? Ultimately, we the public, not just scientists, will have to make these terrible choices. Our view of man and apes will determine our decision.

The Differences between Chimps and Humans

How could just 1.6 percent of genetic difference change chimpanzees into humans? Exactly which genes changed? To answer those questions we need to understand what DNA, our genetic material, does.

Much of our DNA has no known function. Of the DNA that does have known functions, the main functions have to do with proteins, which are long chains of amino acids. Parts of our functional DNA govern the creation of proteins. It works this way: The sequences of small molecules in our DNA specify, or direct, the order of amino acids in our proteins. Certain proteins make up our hair and tissue, while other proteins are enzymes that make and break down the other molecules in our bodies.

The genetic features that are easiest to understand arise from single proteins and single genes, or chunks of DNA. For example, our blood's oxygen-carrying protein, hemoglobin, is made of two amino acid chains, each specified by a single gene. But other genes influence more than one trait. For example, the fatal genetic disease Tay-Sachs causes many visible traits: drooling, abnormal skull growth, yellowish skin, and more. We know that all these effects come from changes in a single enzyme specified by the Tay-Sachs gene, but we don't know how.

Scientists understand the functions of many individual genes that specify individual proteins, but we know much less about how genes shape complex traits, such as behavior. Human hallmarks—that is, characteristics that distinguish us as human—such as art, language, or aggression, are not likely to depend on a single gene. In addition, human behavior is influenced by family, culture, nutrition, and other aspects of each person's environment. It's very controversial what role genes play in the individual differences among humans. But for differences in behavior between *all* chimpanzees and *all* humans, genetic differences are likely to play a role.

The ability of humans but not chimps to speak, for example, must be related to differences in genes that specify the structure of the voice box (larynx) and the wiring of the brain. A young chimpanzee that was raised in a psychologist's home along with the psychologist's daughter of the same age didn't learn to speak or walk upright, although the girl did. Humans grow up to speak, no doubt because of our genetic program. But whether an individual human grows up to speak English or Korean has nothing to do with genes. It depends on what languages the growing child hears spoken.

We don't yet know which chunks of our DNA are responsible for the significant differences between humans and chimps that are covered in the next four chapters. All we can say for sure is that those differences must come from some part of 1.6 percent of our genes. We do know that just one or a few genes can have big impacts. The many big, visible differences between Tay-Sachs patients and those without the disease come from one change in one enzyme.

Cichlid fish, popular for aquariums, also show the impact of small genetic changes. Africa's Lake Victoria has about two hundred species of cichlids. All of them evolved from a single ancestor over a period of about two hundred thousand years. These species differ in their food habits as much as tigers and cows do. Some cichlids graze on algae, some catch insects, some nibble the scales off other fish, some crush snails, and some snatch fish embryos from mother fish. Yet all those species differ from one another by less than half of 1 percent of their DNA. It took fewer genetic mutations to turn a snail crusher into a baby snatcher than it took to produce us from an ape.

CHAPTER 2

THE GREAT LEAP FORWARD

FOR MOST OF THE MILLIONS OF YEARS SINCE
the human line separated from the apes, we
remained little more than glorified chimpanzees. As
recently as sixty thousand years ago, western Europe
was still occupied by Neanderthals, a human species
that scarcely knew of art or progress. Then came an
abrupt change. Anatomically modern humans—that
is, people who looked like us—appeared in Europe,
bringing with them art, musical instruments, trade,
and progress. Soon the Neanderthals were gone.

If there is any one time when it could be said
that we became human, it was at the time of that
Great Leap Forward, sixty thousand years ago.
That leap was probably the result of *another* leap
that took place in Africa and the Middle East. That
earlier leap spanned a few tens of millennia. (One

(left)
Horses, bulls, deer,
and other animals
leap and run on
the walls of a set of
caves in Lascaux,
in southern France.
Created by people
of the Late Ice Age,
around seventeen
thousand years
ago, the prehistoric
artworks of Lascaux
became known to
the modern world
in 1940, when four
teenage boys discov-
ered and explored
the caves.

millennium is a thousand years; ten millennia is ten thousand years.) Even several dozen millennia, though, is a tiny fraction, less than 1 percent, of our long history apart from ape history.

After the Great Leap Forward, we were only a few dozen millennia from domesticating animals, developing agriculture and metalworking, and inventing writing. From there it was a short step to the monuments of civilization, such as the *Mona Lisa*, Beethoven's symphonies, the Eiffel Tower, the International Space Station, and weapons of mass destruction.

What made our sudden, steep rise to humanity possible? What held back the Neanderthals, and what was their fate? Did two species of humans ever meet, and how did they behave toward each other? In short, what made us human, and why did our particular branch on the family tree, *Homo sapiens*, become the last humans standing?

Becoming Human

Life on Earth originated several billion years ago. Dinosaurs became extinct about sixty-five million years ago. It was only between ten and six million years ago that our ancestors became distinct from the ancestors of chimpanzees. Human history is just a tiny percentage of the history of life. Science fiction films that show cavemen running from dinosaurs are just that: science fiction.

The shared ancestor of gorillas, chimps, and humans lived in Africa. Gorillas and chimps are still found only in Africa, and humans remained confined there for millions of years. At first our own ancestors would have been classified as just another species of ape, but a series of three changes launched us in the direction of modern humans.

The first change occurred about four million years ago. Fossils from that time show that our ancestors were regularly walking upright on two legs, unlike gorillas and chimpanzees, which usually walk on four legs and only occasionally on two. When our ancestors began walking upright, their front limbs were freed to do other things—most important, to make tools.

The second change occurred around three million years ago. All modern humans belong to the same species, *Homo sapiens*, but on perhaps several occasions in the past, our lineage—that is, the line of descent leading from our ancestors to us—split into at least two species that lived at the same time. Around three million years ago, our lineage divided into two species. One was a man-ape with a heavy skull and big side teeth. It probably ate coarse plant food. We call that species *Australopithecus robustus*, "the robust southern ape." The other was a man-ape with a thinner, lighter skull and smaller teeth. It probably ate a wide variety of foods. It is called *Australopithecus africanus*, "the southern ape of Africa."

Australopithecus africanus evolved into a larger-brained form called *Homo habilis*, "man the handyman." But *Homo habilis* was not the only branch of our family tree living in Africa several million years ago. We now have fossil evidence that several different species of protohumans, or early forms of humans, existed at that time and place.

The third big change that made our ancestors more human and less apelike was the regular use of stone tools. This is a human trait with clear origins in the animal world. Woodpecker finches, Egyptian vultures, and sea otters are among the other animals that evolved to use tools such as stones or twigs to capture or process food. None of them, though, depend on tools as much as we do.

Common chimpanzees also occasionally use tools, including stone tools, but not so many as to litter the landscape. But by around two and a half million years ago, very crude stone tools appear in large numbers in parts of East Africa where protohumans lived. Since there were multiple protohuman species, who made the tools? Most likely the earliest tools were made by the one protohuman species that survived and kept evolving.

Shakedown in Africa

With two or three protohuman species living in Africa at the same time, but only one human species surviving today, it's clear that some species must have become extinct. Which species survived to become our ancestor?

The winner was the light-skulled *Homo habilis*, who went on to increase in brain size and body size. By 1.7 million years ago enough differences had appeared that scientists give our lineage a new name: *Homo erectus*, "upright-walking man." (*Homo erectus* fossils were found before all the older fossils I've mentioned, so the scientists who named this species didn't yet know that earlier protohumans also walked upright.) Meanwhile, the lineage of *Australopithecus robustus*, the "robust man-ape," disappeared sometime after 1.2 million years ago. Other protohuman species, if any, must have died out around the same time.

Why did the robust man-ape and other protohumans go extinct? Perhaps they could no longer compete with *Homo erectus*, who ate both meat and plants and had tools and a larger brain. It's also possible that *Homo erectus* gave his relatives a push toward extinction by killing them for meat.

The shakedown in Africa left *Homo erectus* as the only protohuman on the stage. By that time *Homo erectus* had already expanded his horizons, starting around two million years ago. His stone tools and bones show that he reached the Middle East, then East Asia. He continued to evolve in our direction, developing a larger brain and a rounder skull. By about half a million years ago, some of our ancestors looked enough like us, and enough different from *Homo erectus*, that they are classified as our own species, *Homo sapiens*, even though they had thicker skulls and heavier bony eyebrow ridges than ours.

Wasn't the appearance of *Homo sapiens* half a million years ago a Great Leap Forward? Not at all. It was a nonevent. Cave paintings, houses, and bows and arrows still lay hundreds of thousands of years in the future. Stone tools continued to be the same crude ones that *Homo erectus* had been making for nearly a million years. The extra brain size of early *Homo sapiens* had no dramatic effect on our way of life. Our rise to humanity was not in direct relation to the changes in our genes. Some vital ingredient still had to be added before the third chimpanzee could come up with the idea of painting the *Mona Lisa*.

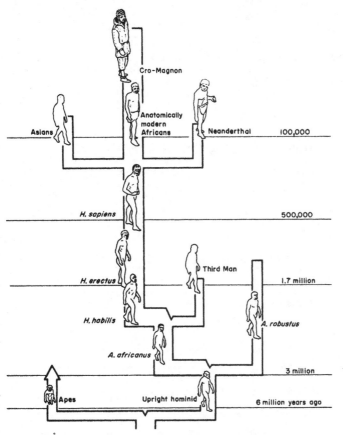

Cro-Magnon

Asians

Anatomically modern Africans

Neanderthal

100,000

H. sapiens

500,000

H. erectus

Third Man

1.7 million

H. habilis

A. robustus

A. africanus

3 million

Apes

Upright hominid

6 million years ago

FIGURE 2

The many-branched human family tree reminds us that for long stretches of prehistory we shared the world with other human species. Our hominid ancestors began evolving separately from apes around 7 million years ago. By 4 million years ago some hominids walked on two legs. Around 3 million years ago, the human line split into two branches, *Australopithecus africanus* and *A. robustus*. The *A. robustus* line died out. The *A. africanus* line split into branches of its own. The *Homo habilis* branch led to *Homo erectus* and later *Homo sapiens*. (Fossils suggest that another branch of *A. africanus*, sometimes called the "Third Man," lived in Africa before dying out.) The *H. sapien* line eventually split into three branches. One branch led to anatomically modern humans in Africa and on to today's global human population. One branch led to the Neanderthals, who became extinct. Scientists are just starting to piece together the history of the third, Asian branch.

MAN, THE NOT-SO-GREAT HUNTER?

HOW DID OUR ANCESTORS MAKE THEIR LIVING during the million and a half years between the appearance of *Homo erectus* and the appearance of *Homo sapiens*?

The only tools from this period are crude stone artifacts. They vary in size and shape. Archaeologists have used these differences to give the tools names such as *hand axe* and *chopper*. In reality, though, these may be just guesses. Wear marks show that all sizes and shapes of tools were used to cut meat, bone, hides, wood, and plants. The tools were not finely made or specialized for particular uses, as later stone tools were.

What food did our ancestors get with these crude tools, and how did they get it? A common image in books about our origins is Man the Hunter. Some anthropologists, the

scientists who study human societies, have suggested that big-game hunting was what led protohumans to cooperate with one another, develop language and big brains, join into bands, and share food.

Western writers and scientists are not the only people with an exaggerated view of hunting. In New Guinea, I lived with real hunters, men who had just recently come out of the Stone Age. At campfires, they talked for hours about hunting. You would think they ate fresh kangaroo meat every day and did little except hunt. But when pressed for details, most admitted that they had bagged only a few kangaroos in their whole lives. One morning I set out with a group of a dozen men armed with bows and arrows. As we passed a fallen tree, the men began shouting. Convinced that an enraged boar or kangaroo was about to come out fighting, I looked for a tree to climb.

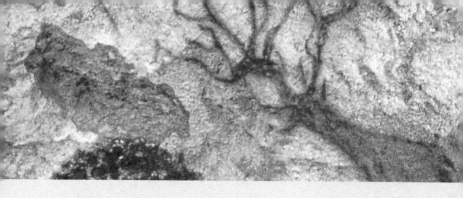

Then I heard triumphant shrieks, and out of the brush came two mighty hunters holding their prey: a pair of baby wrens, barely able to fly. The rest of the day's catch consisted of a few frogs and many mushrooms.

There's no doubt that our early ancestors ate some meat. Their tools left marks on animal bones, and cutting meat from those bones left marks on their tools. But how *much* big-game hunting did they do, and how much of their meat did they get by scavenging the carcasses of animals that were already dead? The oldest really good evidence of human hunting comes from about one hundred thousand years ago—and it's clear that humans then were not yet very effective as hunters. Hundreds of thousands of years earlier, they must have been even worse at it.

Studies of modern hunter-gatherer people—who have far better weapons than early *Homo sapiens* had—show that most of a family's calories come from plant foods gathered by women. Occasionally the men bag a large animal, which contributes significantly to protein intake, but only in the Arctic is big-game hunting the main food source.

I question the usual view that hunting was the driving force behind our uniquely human brain and societies. My guess is that big-game hunting made only small contributions to our diet until *after* we had evolved fully modern anatomy and behavior. For most of our history we were not mighty hunters but skilled chimps, using stone tools to acquire and prepare plants and small animals, bagging big animals only occasionally.

Ice Age Neanderthals

In the period just before the Great Leap Forward, at least three distinct populations of humans lived in different parts of the world. These were the last truly primitive humans, replaced by modern humans at the time of the Great Leap. The best-known of these populations lived in an area that stretched from western Europe through southern Russia and the Middle East to Central Asia. They were the Neanderthals.

The earliest fully Neanderthal skulls and bones date to around 130,000 years ago, although some older bones have features pointing toward the Neanderthals. Most Neanderthal remains come from later than 74,000 years ago. The last Neanderthals died sometime after 60,000 years ago. This means that the Neanderthals flourished when Europe and Asia were in the grip of the last Ice Age. They must have been adapted to life in the cold, but only within limits. They got no farther north than southern Britain, northern Germany, and the Caspian Sea (in Central Asia). The first people to enter Siberia and the Arctic were later, fully modern humans.

Neanderthals' heads were shaped so differently from ours that even in a business suit or designer dress, a Neanderthal would draw stares on the streets of New York or London. Their eyebrows rested on bulging bony ridges, and their noses, jaws, and teeth stuck out farther than the upper part of their faces. Their foreheads were low and slanted, and their lower jaws sloped back without chins. Still, their brains were nearly 10 percent *larger* than ours! They were heavily muscled in their shoulders and necks, and the bones of their arms and legs were thicker than ours. Even their hands were much more powerful than ours. A Neanderthal's handshake would have been literally bone-crushing.

Besides their bones, our main source of information about Neanderthals is their stone tools. Like earlier human tools, Neanderthal tools may have been simple hand-held stones, not mounted on separate parts such as handles. The tools don't fall into distinct types with specialized functions. Some stone blades were undoubtedly used to make wooden tools, but few wooden objects have survived. One exception is an eight-foot-long thrusting spear of wood, found in Germany in the ribs of a long-extinct species of elephant. In spite of that success, though, Neanderthals were probably not very good at big-game hunting. Their numbers were few, and even anatomically modern people living in Africa at the same time as the Neanderthals were not great hunters.

Neanderthals must have built shelters against the cold climate in which they lived, but those shelters must have been crude. All that remains is a few piles of stones and some holes that once held wooden posts, compared with the elaborate remains of houses built later by the Cro-Magnons. Neanderthals must also have worn skins or furs, but they had no needles for sewing fitted garments. They also lacked boats, long-distance trade, and probably art.

Finally, the Neanderthals seem to have lacked that most important human quality, innovation, or the ability to invent new things. We know this because their tools did not vary across time or place. Tools that Neanderthals used in Europe sixty thousand years ago look just like the ones they used a hundred thousand years ago in the Middle East. Despite the Neanderthals' big brains, something was missing.

Yet there are ways in which we can relate to the Neanderthals as human. For one thing, they are the first people to leave clear evidence

An early scientific drawing of ancient stone tools found in southeast England. For a million years or more, such tools were the cutting edge of human technology. Although some have been given labels such as "hand axe," scientists do not know how their makers used them. Sharp-edged blades such as these could have cut through roots and branches, or skins and animal flesh.

that they regularly used fire. Well-preserved Neanderthal caves have small areas of ash and charcoal, signs of simple fireplaces. For another, they may also have been the first people who regularly buried their dead, although the evidence on that point is not yet completely clear.

We do know, though, that Neanderthals took care of the sick and aged people among them. Most skeletons of older individuals show signs of serious physical weaknesses, such as withered arms, missing teeth, and poorly healed broken bones. Only care by young Neanderthals could have kept older ones alive under such conditions. This lets us feel a spark of kinship with these strange creatures of the last Ice Age—nearly human in form and yet not really human in spirit.

Did Neanderthals belong to the same species as we do? That depends on whether a modern human could and would have mated and reared a child with a Neanderthal man or woman. As we will see, there was a chance for that to happen about sixty thousand years ago, at the time of the Great Leap Forward.

The Other Human Populations
The Neanderthals were just one of at least three

humans species occupying different parts of the Old World—the continents of Africa and Eurasia—between one hundred thousand and fifty thousand years ago. Another population lived in eastern Asia. A few fossils from that region show that people there differed from both Neanderthals and modern humans, but we have not yet found enough bones to describe these people in detail.

We know much more about the humans who lived in Africa one hundred thousand years ago. Some of them had skulls very similar in structure to our own. Yet the stone tools of these modern-looking Africans were just like those of the unmodern-looking Neanderthals. These Middle Stone Age Africans, as they are called, still lacked bows and arrows, nets, fishhooks, art, and innovation. Bones that were mostly modern, and also genes that we assume were also mostly modern, were not enough to produce modern human behavior.

Caves occupied by Middle Stone Age Africans give us our first reliable information about what these people ate. Remains found in coastal caves show that they ate seals, penguins, and shellfish. Hunters also captured middle-size animals, especially eland, a kind of antelope. Because eland of all ages were killed, it's possible that hunters managed at times to drive a whole herd of them over a cliff. Bones of more dangerous prey, such as elephants and rhinos, are not found among the food remains. There *are* buffalo bones, but only from very young and very old animals. Middle Stone Age Africans were big-game hunters, but only barely. I suspect that plants and small game made up most of their diet.

By fifty thousand years ago, then, the world had three known human populations: Neanderthals in Europe and western Asia, increasingly modern-looking people in Africa, and a third variety in eastern Asia. The stage was set for the Great Leap Forward. Which population would take the leap?

The Rise of Modern Humans

The evidence for a sudden rise is clearest in France and Spain. There, around sixty thousand years ago, modern humans appeared where before there had been Neanderthals. These people are often called Cro-Magnons, from the name of the French site where their bones were first identified. Their anatomy was like our own.

If a Cro-Magnon dressed in modern clothes strolled down a Paris street, he or she would not stand out from the rest of the crowd in any way.

Archaeologists are as interested in the Cro-Magnons' tools as in their skeletons. The tools suggest that, in Cro-Magnons, modern anatomy was finally joined by modern innovation. These humans of the Late Ice Age made tools in a wide variety of forms, with obvious uses, including needles, fishhooks, mortars and pestles, barbed harpoons, and bows and arrows. Bone and antler tools appeared for the first time. So did compound tools—that is, several pieces tied or glued together, such as axe heads fitted onto wooden handles. By making their cutting tools out of thin blades of stone struck off larger stones, Cro-Magnon toolmakers got ten times more cutting edge than Neanderthals got from the same amount of raw stone.

Late Ice Age sites are much more numerous than those of Neanderthals or Middle Stone Age Africans. The Late Ice Age population must have been significantly larger than the other two groups, which suggests that the people of the Late Ice Age had more success in obtaining food. In fact, they were good big-game hunters.

Many species of big animals that had survived many previous ice ages became extinct at the end of the last Ice Age, possibly exterminated by human hunters' new skills. (We will explore this possibility in more detail in chapters 14 and 15.)

Improved technology also let people occupy new environments, such as Australia, northern Russia, and Siberia. In Europe, people practiced long-distance trade. Modern archaeologists have found tools of high-quality stone, such as obsidian and flint, hundreds of miles from where those stones were quarried. Amber, a form of hardened tree resin used as a gem, reached southern Europe from the shores of the Baltic Sea, in northern Europe. Shells from the Mediterranean reached inland parts of France, Spain, and Ukraine.

The trade in ornamental materials shows that Late Ice Age people had a sense of art and beauty. This relates to the Cro-Magnon achievement we most admire: their art. In addition to covering cave walls with stunning multicolored paintings of now-extinct animals, they carved figurines, jewelry, and musical instruments such as flutes and rattles.

Advances in tools and art did not all appear at the same time. Different innovations appeared in different times and places. Beads and pendants, for example, appeared before cave paintings. Only people in France painted woolly rhinos on cave walls, and only those in Ukraine built houses out of mammoth bones. These variations in culture in time and space are totally unlike the unchanging, universal Neanderthal culture. The variations represent the most important new element in our rise to humanity—the capacity for innovation.

What Happened to the Neanderthals?

Did Neanderthals evolve into Cro-Magnons in Europe? Not likely. The last Neanderthal skeletons, from sometime after sixty thousand years ago, were still fully Neanderthal, while the first Cro-Magnons appearing in Europe at that time were fully modern. Anatomically modern people had been living in Africa and the Middle East tens of thousands of years earlier. It is likely that modern people invaded Europe from that direction rather than evolving in Europe.

What happened when the invading Cro-Magnons met the resident Neanderthals? We can be certain only of the end result. Within a short time, no more Neanderthals.

It seems clear to me that the Cro-Magnon arrival somehow caused the Neanderthal extinction. My guess is that what happened in Europe at the time of the Great Leap Forward was similar to what has happened many times in the modern world whenever a numerous people with advanced technology invades or colonizes the lands of a less-numerous people with less-advanced technology.

When European colonists invaded North America, for instance, most native North Americans died of diseases carried by the invaders. Most of the rest were killed or driven off their land. Some survivors adopted European technology (horses and guns) and resisted for a while. Others were pushed onto land the Europeans didn't want, or else intermarried with them.

Like the Great Plains Indians, who used horses and guns to fight the Europeans, some Neanderthals may have learned Cro-Magnon ways and resisted for a while. What about mating and interbreeding? No convincing skeletal remains that could be considered Neanderthal–Cro-Magnon hybrids are known. If Neanderthal behavior was as primitive as I suspect, and Neanderthals looked as different from Cro-

Magnons as their skeletons suggest, both groups might have had little interest in interbreeding. I think it happened rarely.

We know that it *did* happen in one part of the world, for a short time. Scientists have recently been able to reconstruct Neanderthal DNA and compare it with human DNA. The results show that when modern humans first starting living in the Middle East, some of them interbred with Neanderthals there. As a result, all people alive today appear to have inherited a small amount of their genetic program from the Neanderthals— about 1 percent of our total DNA. After that first small period of interbreeding, there is no evidence that modern humans continued to interbreed with Neanderthals once they moved beyond the Middle East and settled in Europe.

Much of the clearest evidence of the Great Leap Forward comes from western Europe, but modern humans replaced Neanderthals a bit earlier in eastern Europe. In the Middle East, possession of the same area shifted back and forth between Neanderthals and modern humans for about thirty thousand years, between ninety thousand and sixty thousand years ago.

The First Great Leap

The Great Leap Forward really began in Africa. It appears that anatomically modern people arose there more than one hundred thousand years ago. At first, they had the same tools as Neanderthals and had no advantage over them. But by around sixty thousand years ago, some magic twist of behavior had been added to the modern anatomy. That twist produced innovative, fully modern people who spread into the Middle East, Europe, and Asia, replacing the earlier people in those regions.

Two million years ago, several protohuman species lived side by side in Africa until a shakedown left only one. It appears that a similar shakedown among human populations took place within the past sixty thousand years. All of us alive in the world today are descended from the winners of that shakedown. What was the last missing ingredient, the magic twist, that allowed our ancestor to win?

THE LITTLE PEOPLE OF FLORES ISLAND

AN ASTONISHING DISCOVERY ABOUT HUMAN origins was made in 2004. On the island of Flores, in the Southeast Asian nation of Indonesia, researchers unearthed fossil bones of tiny primitive humans. Flores is famous among biologists. It is the home of the world's largest living lizard, the Komodo dragon. It was once the home of a now-extinct species of dwarf elephant. It turns out that, until recently, Flores was also home to humans barely three feet tall, with brains only one-quarter the size of modern human brains—about the size of a chimpanzee's.

Scientists are still debating the meaning of these fossil finds. Some believe that the little people of Flores Island were related to *Homo erectus*, the long-extinct forerunner of humans, and that these relatives of *Homo erectus* lived on for tens of

thousands of years after modern humans arrived in Indonesia. Other scientists think that the fossils might be of modern humans dwarfed by a disease or genetic abnormality, and not of a primitive separate species. My own guess is that the fossils really do represent primitive humans who, like elephants, evolved into a small size after reaching Flores Island, then were quickly exterminated when modern humans arrived. We shall have to see what further discoveries tell us—but the Flores fossils show why it is exciting to live in a time of rapid scientific advances.

A map of the Indonesian Archipelago— can you find the island of Flores?

Tiny Change, Big Leap

The ingredient that produced the Great Leap Forward is an archaeological puzzle without an accepted answer. The missing ingredient doesn't show up in fossil skeletons. It may have been a change in only one-tenth of 1 percent of our DNA. What tiny change in our genes could have had such enormous results?

Like some other scientists who have pondered this question, I can think of only one good answer: language. Anatomical or physical changes made complex spoken language possible. To understand how such a change could trigger a rapid burst of human innovation, take a look at how apes use language.

Chimpanzees, gorillas, and even monkeys are capable of symbolic communication, in which a symbol or a sound represents something else—such as a picture of an apple representing a piece of fruit, or a particular cry meaning "snake!" As we will see in chapter 6, apes have learned to use sign language, plastic symbols, and computers to communicate. Some have mastered "vocabularies" of hundreds of symbols. And wild vervets (or green monkeys) have a natural form of symbolic communication based on grunts, with slightly different grunts to mean "leopard," "eagle," and "snake." If these primates are capable of symbolic communication, why have they not gone on to develop much more complex natural languages of their own?

The answer seems to involve the structure of the larynx (or voice box), the tongue, and all the muscles that give us fine control over spoken sounds. Our ability to speak depends on the perfect functioning of many structures and muscles. If, like apes, we could utter only a few consonants and vowels, our vocabularies would be greatly reduced. The missing ingredient that finally made us fully human could well have been some changes to the protohuman vocal tract—changes that gave us finer control and let us make a much greater variety of sounds. Such small changes to muscle and soft tissue need not show up in fossil skulls.

It's easy to see how a tiny change in anatomy, creating the capacity for speech, would produce a huge change in behavior. With language, it takes only a few seconds to communicate the message, "Turn sharp right at the fourth tree and drive the male antelope toward the red boulder, where I'll spear it." Without language, two protohumans could not brainstorm together about how to organize a hunt or invent a better tool. Without language, even one protohuman would have had difficulty thinking about inventing a better tool.

I don't suggest that the Great Leap Forward began as soon as the mutations for changes in the larynx and tongue appeared. Even with the right anatomy, it must have taken humans thousands of years to develop the structure of language as we know it. But if the missing ingredient did consist of changes that permitted fine control of sounds, then the capacity for innovation would have followed eventually. The spoken word made us free.

Until the Great Leap Forward, human culture had developed at a snail's pace for millions of years. That slow pace was dictated by the pace of genetic change. Our culture and behavior changed only when a mutation occurred to give rise to the change.

After the Great Leap, cultural development no longer depended on genetic change. People could think, innovate, and communicate in a new way. They could pass ideas and knowledge on to other groups and to the next generation. Even though our anatomy has barely changed over the past sixty thousand years, human culture has evolved far more since the Great Leap than in the millions of years before.

Many human cultures have been polygamous. This photograph, taken around 1900, shows Joseph Smith, founder of the Church of Jesus Christ of Latter-Day Saints, or Mormon religion, with his large family, including his children's spouses. Smith had multiple wives, a practice eventually banned by the Mormon Church.

PART TWO

A STRANGE
LIFE CYCLE

OUR EVOLUTION OF LARGE BRAINS AND UPRIGHT posture was needed before we could develop language and art, but it wasn't enough by itself. Human bones don't guarantee humanity. Our rise to humanity also required drastic changes in our life cycle.

Every species has what biologists call a life cycle. It is made up of traits such as the number of offspring produced in each litter or birth, the amount of care that the mother or father gives to the offspring, the way adults form social relationships, how males and females select mates, and how long individuals typically live.

We take the human forms of these traits for granted, as if they were normal. But our life cycle is bizarre by animal standards. To mention just a few examples, most animals produce litters much larger than one baby at a time, most animal fathers provide no parental care to their offspring, and few other animals live even a fraction of seventy years, which is not an unusual life span for a human.

Apes share some of these unusual features. Unlike cats, dogs, songbirds, and goldfish, apes usually have one baby at a time, and they live for several decades. In other ways, however, we're greatly different even from apes. Young chimpanzees are cared for by their mothers, but among humans, most fathers as well as mothers are closely involved in caring for their young. Our infants require a long period of being fed, trained, and protected—a much greater investment of time and energy than ape mothers face. Human fathers who want their children to live and grow up have generally helped their mates raise them.

Our life cycle differs from that of wild apes in other ways. Human females often live for many years after menopause, the point in their lives beyond which they can no longer have children. This is almost unheard of among other mammals. Humans are unusual in their sexual activities, too. Apes engage in sex publicly, in front of other members of their group, and only when the female is ready to bear young. Among humans, sexual activity is usually private, and childbearing is not the only reason for it.

Human society and child-rearing rest on both the skeletal changes mentioned in part 1 and also these remarkable new features of our life cycle. Unlike our skeletal changes, however, our life cycle changes left no fossils. We do know that our life cycle traits have some genetic basis. Among those 1.6 percent of our genes that are different from chimpanzees' genes and that have any function, a significant part is likely to be involved in shaping our life cycle.

Three aspects of our distinctly human life cycle are explored in the next three chapters. The first is human social organization and sexuality. Next is racial variation, the visible differences among humans native to different parts of the globe. I'll argue that these differences arose as a result of the way we humans choose our mates. Finally, I'll ask why we grow old and die. Aging is a part of our life cycle that we take for granted: of course everyone grows old and eventually dies. But why do we *have* to age, when our bodies are able to repair themselves to a great extent?

Here, more than anywhere else in this book, it is important to think in terms of "trade-offs." In the animal world there's nothing that's free or purely good. Everything involves not just benefits but also costs, by using space, time, or energy that could have been devoted to something else. In the framework of evolutionary biology, success is measured in terms of leaving more offspring. As you'll see in chapter 5, this view of success helps explain why it just wouldn't pay for us to make the increased investment in self-repair that we would need to live longer lives. The idea of the trade-off also explains the puzzle of menopause: a shutdown of childbearing so that women can leave *more* surviving children.

CHAPTER 3

HUMAN SEXUALITY

THE HUMAN LIFE CYCLE INCLUDES SEXUALITY
and family life. It is not always easy, though, to
investigate these subjects. One problem is that,
where people's sexual behavior is concerned,
there are limits to the scientific approach. We
can't do controlled experiments the way we can
with diet or teeth-brushing habits. Another is
that the subject can be a sensitive one. Scientists
did not begin to study human sexuality seriously
until recently, and it still can be difficult to view
the subject with a scientific attitude.

Most people regard their relationships
with loved ones—family relationships such
as parent-child ties, and also romantic and
sexual relationships—as deeply meaningful,
personal, and private. It can seem cold-blooded,
even harsh, to put those relationships under a
microscope, so to speak, and look at them with

a scientist's eye. Some people might even be offended to see their interactions with the people in their lives compared with the childrearing behavior of apes or the courtship habits of birds.

As you read this chapter and those that follow, keep two important points in mind. First, we are looking at the human life cycle through the particular framework of evolutionary biology. It does not necessarily explain everything about why people do the things they do—it is simply one of many tools that can help us understand ourselves. Second, our focus is on the entire human species, not on specific examples. There are always many exceptions to every rule, and many people behave very differently than science might predict. Our concern is with general trends, not with people as individuals.

In spite of the challenges of studying human sexuality, we are beginning to understand how it is intertwined with other human characteristics, such as tool use, large brains, and child-rearing practices. Our shift from being just another species of big mammal to being uniquely human involved changes not just in our bones and skulls but also in our family lives and sex lives.

Food and Family Life

To understand how human sexuality got to be the way it is, we have to understand the evolution of our diet and our society. From the vegetarian diet of our ape ancestors, we separated within the last several million years to eat meat as well as plant foods, yet our teeth and claws remained those of apes, not of tigers. Instead of on teeth and claws, our success in hunting depended on large brains. By using tools and hunting in organized groups, our ancestors could hunt, and they regularly shared food with one another. We started using tools to gather roots and berries as well, so even the vegetarian part of our diets required large brains.

Human children took years to acquire the information and experience they needed to be efficient hunter-gatherers, just as today they take years to learn how to be farmers or computer programmers. For many years after they are weaned—after they stop nursing on milk from the mother's body and start to eat food—they are too ignorant and helpless to take care of themselves. Human children depend on parents to bring food to them. This seems natural to us, but it is exceptional in the primate world. Baby apes gather food for themselves as soon as they are weaned.

Human infants are terrible food gatherers for two reasons. One reason is mechanical. Making and using the tools needed to find food requires fine finger coordination that children take years to develop. Just as my sons couldn't tie their shoelaces when they were four years old, four-year-old hunter-gatherer children can't sharpen a stone axe or build a dugout fishing canoe.

The second reason is mental. More than other animals, we depend on brainpower when we look for food, because we have a much more varied diet and more complicated food-gathering techniques. New Guineans whom I work with typically have separate names for about a thousand different plant and animal species in their vicinity. For each species, they know something about where to find it, whether it is edible or useful, and how to capture or harvest it. All this information takes years to acquire.

Weaned human infants not only need adults to feed them; they need adults to teach them for a decade or two. As with so many human hallmarks, these needs occur in other species. Young lions, for example, must be taught how to hunt by their parents. Chimpanzees, like humans, have a varied diet and use a number of

(right)
Family life in the species *Homo sapiens* is organized around a simple fact: human children cannot fend for themselves at birth or for a long time afterward. They need parental care, not just for food, shelter, and protection, but to learn the skills they will need to survive in society.

techniques to obtain food. Chimpanzee parents do help their young find food, and common chimps also make some use of tools, although bonobos do not. But for humans, the necessary survival skills, and the burden on the parents, are much greater than for lions or chimps.

That parental burden means that care by the father as well as the mother is important if the child is to survive. Orangutan fathers provide their offspring with nothing. Gorilla, chimpanzee, and gibbon fathers do more, providing some protection for their young. Human hunter-gatherer fathers do even more, providing some food and much teaching. Our complex food-gathering habits require a social system in which a male has a long-term relationship with a female, so that he can help rear their child. Otherwise the child will be less likely to survive, and the father will be less likely to pass on his genes.

A Social System That Meets Our Needs

The orangutan system, in which the father simply departs as soon as he and his female partner have mated, wouldn't work for us. The chimpanzee system also wouldn't work for us. Among chimpanzees, a female who is ready to be fertilized and become pregnant is likely to mate with several adult males within a short time. As a result, a chimpanzee male has no idea which infants in the troop he has fathered. This is no big loss to a chimp father, because males don't do a great deal for the troop infants. A human father, though, spends a lot of time and energy on the care of his child. From the point of view of evolution, a human male had better have some confidence that the child is his, or his child care contributions may help pass on some other man's genes.

Confidence about fatherhood would be no problem if humans, like gibbons, were scattered across the landscape in isolated couples, so that a female almost never saw a male other than her mate. Almost all human populations, however, have consisted of groups of adults. Hunting and gathering often involve cooperative group efforts among men, women, or both. Groups also offer protection against predators and enemies, especially other humans.

To meet our need for both confidence in fatherhood *and* group living, humans evolved a social system that seems normal to us, although it is strange by ape standards. Adult orangutans are solitary. Adult gibbons live as solitary male-female pairs. Gorillas live in harems consisting of several adult females and usually one dominant adult male. Common chimpanzees live in communities of scattered females plus a group of males, in which individuals mate with more than one partner. Pygmy chimps, or bonobos, form colonies of both sexes that are even more promiscuous, meaning that individuals have multiple sex partners.

Human societies resemble none of these primate societies. Like our food habits, our social system resembles more that of lions or wolves. We live in bands containing many adult males and females. Among lions, however, any male can and does mate with any female, meaning that the fatherhood of lion cubs is unknowable. Among humans, males and females are paired off with each other. The closest thing to our social system in the animal world is large colonies of seabirds, such as gulls and penguins, which also organize into male-female pairs.

Officially, at least, in most modern political states human pairing is more or less monogamous, meaning that each individual has a single partner. Among hunter-gatherer bands, which are better models for how humans lived over the last million years, most men can support only a single family, but a few powerful men have several wives. The huge harems some human rulers have maintained weren't possible until the rise of agriculture and centralized government let a few princes tax everyone else to feed the royal harem's babies.

Why Men Are Bigger Than Women

Adult men are, on average, slightly bigger than women of the same age. Although there are many individual exceptions, across a whole population men weigh about 20 percent more than women and are about 8 percent taller. Why is this the case? The answer lies in our social and sexual organization.

The typical hunter-gatherer social system, in which most men have one partner but a few men have several wives, can be called "mildly polygynous." (*Polygynous* means "with multiple wives.") Because humans were hunter-gatherers for many millennia before the rise of agriculture, that particular social organization explains why men are bigger than women.

Among polygynous mammals, the average difference in size between males and females

is related to the number of females that mate with a single male, and only with that male. The more females in a male's harem, the greater the size difference between the sexes. The biggest harems are seen in species with males much larger than females. Three examples from the animal world show how this works.

Gibbons are monogamous. Each individual has only one partner. The male gibbon has no harem, and there is no average size difference between the sexes. Males and females are the same size. Male gorillas, on the other hand, typically have harems of three to six wives. This is reflected in a size difference: a male weighs about twice as much as a female. The average harem of a southern elephant seal is forty-eight females. With such a big harem size, you would expect a big difference in size between the sexes, and you would be right. A three-ton (six-thousand-pound) male seal dwarfs his seven-hundred-pound wives.

The explanation is that in a monogamous species, every male has the opportunity to win a female. In a very polygynous species, such as the elephant seal, many males go without mates, because a few dominant males have succeeded in rounding up all the females into

(left)
Surrounded by his harem of smaller females, a large male elephant seal basks on the not-so-balmy beach of King George Island, Antarctica.

their harems. The bigger the harem, the fiercer the competition among males—and the more important it is for a male to be big, because the bigger male generally wins a fight.

We humans, with our slightly bigger males and slight polygyny, fit this pattern. At some point in human evolution, though, male intelligence and personality came to count for more than size. Big men don't tend to have more wives than smaller ones.

Our Unusual Sex Lives

Human sexual activity is freakish by the standards of other mammals. For one thing, most mammals are sexually inactive most of the time. They copulate, or engage in sex, only when the female is estrous. That means that she has entered estrus, the part of her biological cycle when she is ovulating—her ovaries are preparing to release an egg. During this time she can be fertilized and become pregnant.

Depending upon the species, females enter estrus at various time intervals, from every few weeks to a few times a year. Females of some species enter estrus just once a year. Then and only then are they willing to copulate with males, and they advertise this fact to males through behavior and, sometimes, changes in their appearance.

Human sexual cycles are quite different. Instead of being limited to a short estrus phase, a sexually mature woman, like a man, may choose to engage in sexual activity whenever she decides to do so. Women ovulate once a month, but unlike other primate females, they do not advertise this fertile phase to males with changes in their appearance or behavior. In fact, human ovulation is so well concealed, from women as well as men, that doctors only began to understand its timing in the 1930s.

Concealed ovulation, together with the fact that women have the ability to be sexually active when they want and not just during the time of the month when they are fertile, means that most sexual encounters by humans are at the wrong time for conceiving a child. Whatever the main biological function of human sex might be, it isn't to produce children. In no species besides humans has sex become so unconnected to conception.

For animals, copulation is a dangerous luxury. Animals in the act of mating burn energy and neglect opportunities to obtain food. They are also vulnerable to predators who want to eat them or rivals who want to take over their territory. Copulation is something to be accomplished in the minimum time needed for fertilization.

If we regarded human sex as a means of achieving fertilization, it would be a colossal failure in evolutionary terms. It gets the job done, but it consumes a great deal of time and energy, because humans engage in much sexual activity at times when fertilization is impossible or unlikely. If we had kept an estrus cycle like other mammals, including our close primate relatives, our hunter-gatherer ancestors could have spent that wasted time butchering more mastodons and gathering more berries.

The most hotly debated question in the evolution of human sexuality is how we wound up with concealed ovulation, and what good all those mistimed copulations do us. Sex is pleasurable, but evolution made it that way. If our species weren't getting some evolutionary benefit from our sexual activities, the world would have been taken over by mutant humans who evolved not to enjoy sex.

Closely related to the question of concealed ovulation is that of concealed copulation. All other animals that live in groups—whether individuals are monogamous or have multiple partners—copulate in full view of the other animals in their group. Why are humans unique in our strong preference for keeping our sexual activity private?

Biologists are currently arguing over theories to explain the origin of concealed ovulation and copulation in humans. From an evolutionary point of view, some factor or combination of factors caused us to evolve these traits in the distant past. The traits would not still be present today if some factors weren't keeping them alive. The factors responsible for concealed ovulation and copulation today don't necessarily *have* to be the same factors that caused those traits to appear in the first place. Three of the explanations biologists have suggested for the origin of our unusual sex lives, however, seem to me to be still in operation today.

Those explanations are:

* Concealed ovulation and copulation evolved to reduce aggression and increase cooperation among males;
* Concealed ovulation and copulation strengthen the bonds between particular

couples, laying the foundations of the human family; and

* Women evolved concealed ovulation to encourage men to bond permanently with their partners, which in turn makes men more confident that they are the fathers of the children their partners bear.

All these explanations reflect a key feature of human social organization. A man and woman who want their child (and their genes) to survive must cooperate with each other for a long time to rear that child. At the same time, they must cooperate economically with other couples living close by. Regular sexual relations between the man and woman create a bond that is closer than the couple's ties to their friends and neighbors. These close bonds between couples are a kind of social cement, not just a mechanism of fertilization. Our sex lives take place in private to emphasize the difference between sexual and nonsexual partners within the same close group.

The Science of Adultery
The human mating system is based on male and female pairs that rear children together and

form a lasting bond. Another primate species also forms lasting pairs: the little apes called gibbons. Their mating system is different from that of humans, however. Gibbon couples live alone, apart from other gibbons, not in groups or communities. Gibbons who have formed a pair bond do not have sex outside the bond.

Humans live in social groups, not solitary pairs. They also, at times, engage in sexual activity with people other than their partners. Sexual activity by married people outside their marriage, called adultery or extramarital sex, is an exception to our "normal" pattern of married sex.

Adultery can be a heartbreaking, life-wrecking matter. Why, then, do humans do it? Like other behaviors, adultery can be examined from the point of view of evolution. Remember that when we use the framework of evolutionary biology, we look at patterns across whole species, and evolution is only one of the forces that drive human behavior.

If life is viewed as an evolutionary contest, the winners are those who leave the greatest number of offspring. Different species have different strategies for winning the contest. Some species are purely monogamous, others are highly promiscuous (meaning that individuals may mate with many partners), and some follow a mixed strategy: monogamous, with exceptions.

Within any species, the best strategy for males may not be the same as the best strategy for females. That is the case with humans. For men, the minimum effort needed to produce an offspring is copulation, which requires only a little time and energy. For women, the minimum effort is copulation plus nine months of pregnancy—and, throughout most of human history, several years of nursing as well. That's a huge investment of time and energy. As a result, a man can potentially produce far more offspring in his lifetime than a woman can. The record lifetime number of offspring for a man is 888, sired by Emperor Ismail the Bloodthirsty of Morocco. The record for a woman is 69 children, born to a nineteenth-century Russian woman who had multiple sets of triplets. Few women have topped twenty children, while some men in polygynous societies easily do so.

This biological difference means that a man can potentially gain much more from extramarital sex than a woman can—*if* the only measure of success is the number of offspring.

That could be one reason a man might seek sex outside marriage. Why would a woman? Research in many parts of the world suggests that women's motives for sex outside marriage often include dissatisfaction with their marriages and a desire to find a new lasting relationship.

Does all this mean that extramarital sex is "only natural" and should be accepted? Not at all. Understanding and explaining a behavior is not the same thing as defending or accepting it. The goal of all human activity can't be reduced to an evolutionary drive. We humans are able to choose other goals. Many people are simply not interested in relationships with people other than their partners. For others, goals such as honoring a promise to be faithful to one's partner, staying true to religious and moral beliefs, or protecting the family are stronger than the urge to engage in extramarital sex. Among our species, success and happiness are not measured only by the number of offspring we leave. For evidence, consider the fact that many successful and happy women and men choose to limit their family size, or not to have children. Consider also that many humans form same-sex bonds, or have gender identities beyond traditional male and female roles.

MONOGAMOUS BIRDS—OR ARE THEY?

IN THE ANIMAL WORLD, THE CLOSEST MATCH to the human mating system is found in the nesting colonies of certain birds. Herons and gulls, for example, breed and rear their young in dense colonies of male-female pairs that appear monogamous. Successful chick rearing calls for two parents. One bird cannot raise a chick alone, because an unguarded nest will probably be destroyed while the parent is off gathering food, and a male cannot feed and guard two nests at the same time.

In a study of great blue herons and great egrets in Texas, observers watched males who were left guarding their nests while their mates went off to find food. For the first day or two after pairing with their mates, the males often courted other passing females, although they did not copulate with them. The courting seemed to be a kind of "insurance," in which a male tried to line up a backup mate in case his female deserted him (which happens in 20 percent of cases). The passing "backup" female is a

single bird seeking a mate. She does not know the male already has a mate until his spouse returns to chase her away. Eventually the male gains complete confidence that his spouse will not desert him, and he stops courting the passing females.

Herring gulls follow a different strategy. A study of these birds in Lake Michigan found that 35 percent of the mated males engaged in extramarital sex. All mated female gulls, however, rejected the advances of males other than their mates, and they never flirted with neighboring males when their mates were away. All the male gulls who committed "adultery" did so with single females. At the same time, these males were "good providers"—they brought their mates plenty of food.

Studies such as these have shown that so-called "monogamous" birds are not always monogamous. In some species, adulterous males try to have it both ways: keeping their spouses faithful while siring offspring with other females.

(above)
Ardea herodias, or great blue herons, and their nests.

A Choice among Goals

We are not mere slaves to the traits we have evolved, not even to those encoded in our genes. Modern civilization is fairly successful at ending ancient behaviors such as stealing brides from rival tribes or murdering children. While the evolutionary viewpoint is valuable for understanding how human social and sexual practices originated, it is not the only way to understand the way we behave today.

Once human culture was firmly in place, it acquired new goals. Questions of sexual faithfulness or promiscuity are not decided simply by our evolutionary heritage. They are also ethical questions, involving our ideas and beliefs about right and wrong behavior. Like other animals, we evolved to win at the contest of leaving as many descendants as possible, but we have also chosen to pursue ethical goals, which can direct our behavior in different ways. Having that choice among goals is one of the biggest differences between us and other animals.

How We Pick Our Mates

One final piece of the puzzle that is human sexuality concerns the mystery of attraction.

What draws us to one possible partner instead of another? How do we choose our mates?

Psychologists have tackled this question by examining many married couples, measuring everything conceivable about them and then trying to make sense out of who married whom. Not surprisingly, most husbands and wives turn out to share the same ethnic background (although racially and ethnically mixed marriages are on the rise), religious beliefs, and political views. Spouses also tend to match each other reasonably well in intelligence and in personality qualities such as neatness.

What about physical appearance? It turns out that if you measure enough couples, you make an unexpected discovery. There are many exceptions, but *on average*, spouses resemble each other slightly—but enough to be statistically significant—in almost every physical feature. This is true for the obvious physical features we think of first when describing people: height, weight, and color of eyes, hair, and skin. But it is also true for dozens of less obvious traits, such as breadth of nose, length of earlobe or middle finger, distance between eyes or around the wrist, and lung volume!

Experimenters have made this finding for people as far apart as Poles in Poland, Americans in Michigan, and Africans in Chad. In each case, spouses were not identical, but they were more alike than they would have been if they had been randomly paired.

In spite of the old saying "opposites attract," people on average tend to marry people who are more like them than they are different. One reason for this is that we tend to spend a lot of time around people who are similar to us. Many people live in neighborhoods defined by ethnic background, or religion, or social and economic status. We meet people of the same religion in church. Family friends often share our own family's interests, political views, and social and economic status.

Those contacts give us many opportunities to meet and fall in love with someone similar to ourselves. But we don't live in neighborhoods grouped by length of earlobe, so there must be some other reason spouses tend to be matched that way, too. The answer lies in physical attraction based on appearance. All kinds of traits—the obvious ones such as height and hair color, and the less obvious ones such as earlobe length and eye spacing—come together to form a search image, a mental picture of our ideal mate. We may not be consciously aware that we *have* such an image, but it is what makes us feel that "He's my type" or "She's not my type" when we meet someone new.

We are attracted to people who look somewhat like us because our search images are based on people who share half our genes: our parents and siblings. We begin to develop our search image of a future partner when we are very young, between birth and age six. The image is heavily influenced by the people of the opposite sex whom we see most often. For most of us, that's our mother or father, sister or brother, and close childhood friends.

We may have evolved to form an early search image of the ideal mate, but researchers have found time and time again that factors such as personality, intelligence, and religion have more influence than physical appearance on our choice of spouses. Like other aspects of our social and sexual lives, our feeling of attraction to possible romantic partners, and our eventual choice of partners, whether of the opposite sex or our own, is driven only partly by our evolutionary heritage. It is also determined by our life experiences, values, and goals.

CHAPTER 4

THE ORIGIN OF HUMAN RACES

IMAGINE YOU WERE INTRODUCED TO THREE people: one each from Nigeria, Japan, and Sweden. You would probably have no trouble deciding at a glance which person came from which country. You'd see differences in skin color, the color and shape of eyes, the color and texture of hair, and general body size and shape. These differences would point to different continents of origin: Africa for the Nigerian, Asia for the Japanese, and Europe for the Swede. A trained anthropologist might be able to do better, placing each person in the right part of his or her country.

Human features vary with geography, creating racial variations. Since scientists have answered so many highly technical questions about obscure species of plants and animals,

(left, pages 95 and 96) Whatever their style, people more often than not choose mates who resemble them. Any new style can catch on—if enough potential dating and mating partners find it attractive.

you might expect them to have answered one of the most obvious questions about us: Why do people from different areas look different? Our understanding of how humans came to differ from other animals would be incomplete if we did not consider how, in the process, human populations became visibly different.

The subject of human races, however, is an explosive one. British scientist Charles Darwin shied away from it in his 1859 book *On the Origin of Species*, which introduced the world to the ideas that form the foundation of modern biology. Even today, few scientists dare to study racial origins, for fear they will be called racists just for being interested in the subject.

Another reason we don't understand the meaning of racial variations is that it's an unexpectedly difficult problem. Darwin's own theory was that human races originated because of sexual selection—in other words, the mating choices people make. To this day, that theory is controversial. Modern biologists usually argue that racial origins came about through a different process, called natural selection. Yet they can't even agree how natural selection might have led to features such as dark skin in the tropics, to take just one example of racial variation.

In this chapter we'll look at the two forces that have been suggested as the source of racial variations: natural selection and sexual selection. You'll see that I think natural selection played only a secondary role, and that sexual selection has been the primary shaper of human racial variation.

Visible Variations

Racial variation is not confined to humans. Most animal and plant species that are distributed over wide areas, including gorillas and common chimpanzees, also vary geographically. This means that populations of the same species living in different parts of the species' range have recognizable, visible differences.

How can we decide whether two recognizably different populations, from different places, belong to the same species? If no interbreeding occurs naturally when they come into contact, they are separate species. If interbreeding does occur, they belong to the same species, but because of their differences, they can be considered separate races (also known as subspecies) within that species. All gorillas, for example, belong to a single species. Within that species are three races, or subspecies, of gorillas: mountain, eastern lowland, and western lowland. They are set apart by visible differences in body size, hair length, and hair color.

Closely related species that occasionally interbreed in captivity, such as tigers and lions, remain separate species because they do not interbreed in the wild. All humans, in contrast, belong to the same species, because some interbreeding has taken place whenever any two human populations have come into contact.

Racial variation has characterized humans for at least the past several thousand years, and possibly much longer. Writing around 450 BC, the Greek historian Herodotus described black-skinned Ethiopians from Africa and a red-haired, blue-eyed tribe from Russia. Ancient paintings, mummies from Egypt and Peru, and bodies preserved in European peat bogs show that several thousand years ago, people differed in their hair and faces as much as they do today. Fossils show that by at least ten thousand years ago, skulls of people from various parts of the world were different, in ways similar to the racial variations in skull shape that anthropologists see in people today.

Does Natural Selection Explain Skin Color?

Now let's turn to the question of how our visible geographic differences originated. One argument is that they are the result of natural selection, a mechanism that drives evolution, the pattern of change in life forms over time, as new species develop from earlier ones. Natural selection simply means that genetic traits that help a plant or animal survive get passed on to that organism's offspring.

New traits arise, or existing traits change, when changes occur in genes because of random mutations. Genetic changes are just as likely to harm an individual plant or animal, or to have no effect on it, as they are to help it. But if the mutation *does* help the organism—if it leads to a slightly longer bill, say, that lets a bird pick more beetles out of tree bark—that organism is likely to live longer than others of its species, which means that it can have more offspring. Those offspring will inherit its genetic program, including the new mutation. They will have the survival advantage that the mutation brought, and *their* offspring will spread it more widely. In time, the mutation becomes established in a population, resulting in a new subspecies or even a whole new species.

Natural selection accounts for many differences between species, such as the fact that lions have paws with claws while we have grasping fingers. Natural selection also explains some racial or geographic variation within species. For example, Arctic weasels that live in areas covered by winter snow change color from brown in summer to white in winter, while weasels that live farther south stay brown all year. That racial difference improves the weasels' survival. White weasels would be glaringly easy to see against a brown background, but against snow they are camouflaged and less obvious to their prey.

Natural selection surely explains *some* geographic variation in humans. For example, many Africans but no Swedes have the sickle cell hemoglobin gene, because that gene protects against malaria, a tropical disease that occurs in Africa but not in Sweden. Other localized human traits that must have evolved through natural selection include the big chests of

Indians in the Andes Mountains of South America (good for getting oxygen from thin air at high altitudes) and the compact shapes of Eskimos (good for saving heat in a cold climate).

Can natural selection explain the racial differences that we think of first—skin color and eye color? If so, we might expect that the same trait, such as blue eyes, would reappear in parts of the world with similar climates, and that scientists would agree on what the trait is good for.

Skin color should be the easiest trait to understand. Our skins run the spectrum from various shades of black, brown, copper, and yellowish to pink with or without freckles. The usual story to explain this variation by natural selection goes like this: People from sunny Africa have black skin. So do people from other sunny areas, such as southern India and New Guinea. Skin gets paler as you move north or south away from the equator, until you reach northern Europe, where you find the palest skin of all. Obviously, dark skin evolved in people who were exposed to a lot of sunlight, because dark skin protects against sunburn and skin cancer. Doesn't that make sense?

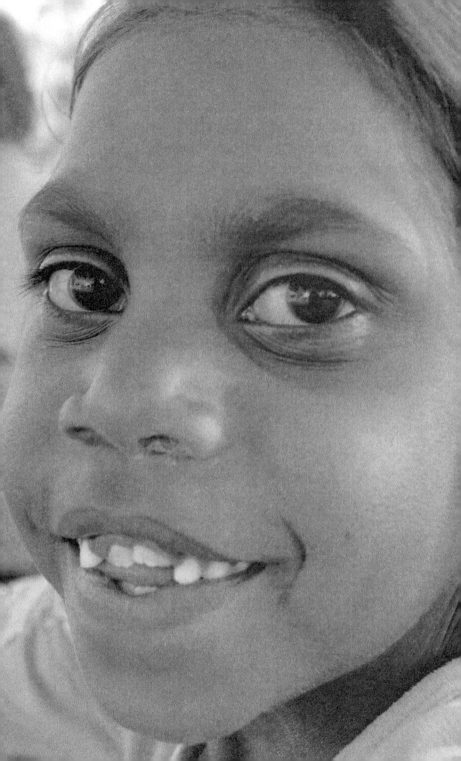

Unfortunately, it's not so simple. To begin with, sunburn and skin cancer cause very few deaths compared with infectious diseases. This means that sunburn and skin cancer would not be powerful pressures for natural selection. At least eight other theories have been suggested to explain why natural selection could have favored dark skin in the tropics and pale skin in the north. Among these theories: dark skin provides camouflage in the jungle, and pale skin is less sensitive to frostbite.

But the biggest objection to any of these theories is that the link between dark skin and sunny climates is not perfect. Native peoples evolved dark skin in some areas with relatively little sunlight, such as the forested Australian island of Tasmania, while in sunny areas of tropical Southeast Asia, skin color is only medium. No American Indians have black skin, even in the sunniest regions. In the Solomon Islands of the Pacific, jet-black people and lighter-skinned people live on islands that share the same climate conditions.

Anthropologists argue that some light-skinned tropical people migrated to their sunny regions too recently to have evolved dark skin. The ancestors of

(*left*)
In some parts of Australia, more than three-quarters of Aboriginal children have light blond hair, although it sometimes turns brown as they grow up. The other population in which blond hair is common is pale-skinned northern Europeans.

American Indians may have reached the Americas just eleven thousand years ago—perhaps not long enough to evolve black skin in the hot American tropics. To support the climate theory of skin color, anthropologists also point out that Scandinavians, who have pale skin, live in the cold, dark, foggy North. The problem is that Scandinavians have been in northern Europe for only four or five thousand years—even less time than American Indians have been in the Amazon. Either Scandinavians acquired their pale skin long ago in some other place, or they evolved it in less than half the time that American Indians have lived in the Amazon *without* evolving black skin.

If the link between skin color and climate seems weak, there appears to be no link at all between climate and the color of hair or eyes. Blond hair is common in cold, wet, Scandinavia and also among Aborigines of the hot, dry center of Australia. What do these two areas have in common, and how could blond hair help both Swedes and Aborigines to survive?

Sexual Selection and Physical Appearances
When Darwin considered the problem of human geographic variations, he decided that natural

selection had nothing to do with it. He came up with a theory he preferred: sexual selection.

Darwin had noticed that many animals have features with no obvious survival value, such as the long, colorful tails of male peacocks and the dark, shaggy manes of male lions. These features do help animals get mates, however, either by attracting individuals of the opposite sex or by intimidating rivals. Male peacocks and lions that are especially successful at attracting females and scaring off rivals will leave more descendants than other males. Their genes will get passed on, and those genes will spread through a population because of sexual selection, or mating preferences, not because of natural selection. The same argument applies to female traits as well.

For sexual selection to work, evolution must produce two changes at the same time. One sex must evolve a trait, and the other sex must evolve a liking for that trait. Male peacocks could hardly afford to flash their fancy tails if the sight revolted females and drove them away. As long as one sex has it and the other sex likes it, sexual selection could lead to just about any trait, if that trait doesn't interfere too much with survival.

Could human variations such as skin color be the result of sexual preferences that just happen to vary from place to place? Darwin believed the answer was yes. He noted that people in different parts of the world define beauty in terms of what is familiar to them. Individuals on the Pacific island of Fiji, or among the Bushmen of southern Africa, or in Iceland grow up learning the local standards of beauty. These standards tend to live on in each population because individuals who match them closely have the greatest success in finding mates and passing on their genes to offspring.

Darwin died before his theory of sexual selection could be tested against studies of how people actually choose their mates. As we saw in the last chapter, plenty of such studies have now taken place. They show that, on the whole, people tend to marry individuals who resemble them in many features, including skin, hair, and eye color. Our beauty standards are based on people we see around us in childhood, especially our parents and siblings, whom we see the most—and who resemble us most closely, since we share their genes.

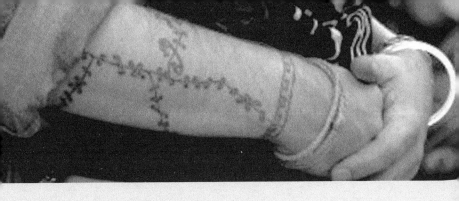

WHITE, BLUE—AND PINK?

WE APPEAR TO CHOOSE OUR MATES BASED on standards of beauty that we imprint on, or form an attachment to, early in our lives. For a strong test of the imprinting theory of mate choice, we would have to do some experiments. And while it is not practical or possible to do such experiments with people, we can do them with animals.

One study involved snow geese. These birds occur in the wild in either of two colors, called the white phase and the blue phase. Canadian researchers wanted to know if snow geese are born with an inherited preference for white or blue mates, or if they learn which phase to prefer as they grow up. They hatched goose eggs in an incubator, then placed the goslings, or infant geese, with foster parents. When these infants grew up, they preferred mates of the same color as their foster parents. But

goslings that grew up in a mixed flock of both blue and white birds showed no preference for one color of mate over another.

As a final touch, the biologists dyed some of the white parent geese pink, a color that does not occur in nature! Goslings raised by these parents came to prefer pink-dyed geese as mates. This showed that geese do not inherit their color preference. They learn it in childhood, by imprinting on their parents, siblings, and playmates.

Traits, Tastes, and Mating Choices

How do I think people in different parts of the world evolved their differences? Our insides are invisible to us, so they were molded only by natural selection. This is why tropical Africans, but not Swedes, got the antimalaria defense of the sickle cell hemoglobin gene. Many visible features on our outside also got molded by natural selection. But just as in animals, sexual selection had a big effect on molding the visible traits by which we are attracted to our mates.

For us humans, those traits include especially the skin, hair, and eyes. In each part of the world, those traits developed in lockstep with our imprinted preferences, the tastes and ideals of beauty that form when we are young. The traits reinforced the preferences, and the preferences reinforced the traits. The result was different color packages in different parts of the world.

Which particular human population ended up with a given eye or hair color may have been partly an accident of what biologists call the "founder effect." This means that if a few individuals colonize an empty land, and their descendants multiply and fill the land, the genes of those few founding individuals may still dominate in the population generations later.

I don't mean to say that climate has nothing to do with skin color. Tropical peoples tend on average to have darker skin than those who live farther from the equator (although there are many exceptions). This is probably due to natural selection, even though we are not sure exactly how. I am saying that sexual selection has been strong enough to make any link between skin color and sun exposure quite imperfect.

If you doubt the idea that traits and preferences can evolve together to different end points, consider fashion. In the 1950s, right after World War II, women favored men with crew cuts and clean-shaven faces. Since then we've seen a parade of men's fashions, including beards, long hair, earrings, and purple-dyed Mohawks. A young man who dared to flaunt any of those fashions in the 1950s would have revolted the girls and had zero mating success. In more recent times, however, those looks have gained appeal within some populations, where they are preferred by females. This is not because short hair was especially suited to the climate of the 1950s, while Mohawks aid survival today. It's because men's appearances and women's tastes evolved together, far faster than any evolutionary change, since no gene mutations were needed. The same thing happens with female fashions.

The visible geographic variability that sexual selection has produced in humans is impressive. I don't know of any other wild animal species in which the eye color of different populations can be green, blue, gray, brown, or black, while skin color varies geographically from pale to black and hair is either red, yellow, brown, or black. There may be no limits to the colors with which sexual selection can adorn us, except the time required by evolution. Twenty thousand years from now there might be women with naturally green hair and red eyes—and men who think they are gorgeous.

CHAPTER 5

WHY DO WE GROW OLD AND DIE?

IS THERE A BELOVED GRANDPARENT IN YOUR life? Or maybe a respected teacher? You can probably think of at least one older person who has enriched your life.

We enter life surrounded by people who are older than we are: our parents, grandparents, aunts and uncles, and maybe older brothers and sisters. They become our protectors, guides, families, and friends. We cherish our relationships with these loved ones. It is hard to accept the fact that we will lose them someday, but life naturally draws to an end as old age is followed by death. It is a fate that all of us will eventually share.

Like members of every other species on earth, individuals of our species, *Homo sapiens*, have a life expectancy that is a feature of our life

(*left*)
Spanish soldier and military governor Juan Ponce de León explored Florida in 1513. Later, some historians claimed that he was searching for the Fountain of Youth, a mythical spring whose waters cured disease and granted eternal life. Some scientists still hope to find the secret of endless—or at least longer—life.

cycle. Life expectancy is the term scientists use to describe the average period that a member of any species can expect to live. Many factors influence life expectancy. For humans, a key factor is where you live. People born in different countries may have different life expectancies, based on things such as the quality of the food, water, and medical care available to them. The life expectancy for adults in the United States is now seventy-six years for men and almost eighty-one years for women. Few of us, though, will survive to one hundred.

Why is it so easy to live almost 80 years, so hard to live 100, and almost impossible to survive to 120? Why do humans with access to the best medical care, and animals kept in a cage with plenty of food and no predators, inevitably grow weak or sick and die? Death is one of the most obvious features of our life cycle, but there's nothing obvious about what causes it.

Slow Aging

We age more slowly than our closest relatives. Not a single ape of any species has been recorded as achieving the current life expectancy of American humans. Only exceptional apes reach their fifties. Some of our slow aging may have developed fairly recently in our evolutionary history, around the time of the Great Leap Forward, sixty thousand years ago. Few Neanderthals survived past the age of forty. Among the Cro-Magnons who replaced them, quite a few lived into their sixties.

Slow aging is vital to the human life cycle, which depends on shared information. As language evolved, we became able to pass on far more information than before. Today we can pass it in written or recorded form, but writing is a fairly recent development in our history. For tens of thousands of years before writing, old people were our libraries. They served as keepers of a group's shared information and experience, just as they continue to do in tribal societies today. Under hunter-gatherer conditions, the knowledge possessed by even one seventy-year-old could mean the difference between starvation and survival for a whole clan.

Our ability to survive to a ripe old age had something to do with our advances in culture and technology. It's easier to defend yourself against a lion with a spear than with a hand-held stone, easier still with a high-powered rifle. But advances in culture and technology would not have been enough to give us longer lives unless our bodies had also been redesigned to last longer. As we'll see in this chapter, our biology became remolded to match the increased life expectancy made possible by our cultural and technological advances.

Aging is studied by two groups of scientists who take very different approaches. Physiologists explore the body and its structures, searching for the mechanisms within our cells that bring about aging. Evolutionary biologists try to understand how natural selection could ever permit aging to occur. I think that aging can't be understood unless we seek both explanations. I expect that the evolutionary explanation (why we age) will help us find the physiological explanation (what specific features and processes in our bodies cause us to age).

Repair and Replace

Physiologists tend to think that something about our bodies and their systems makes aging unavoidable. One theory is that aging occurs because our immune systems find it harder and harder to tell the difference between our own cells and foreign cells from outside our bodies. This is a fatal defect in our immune systems. Could natural selection have created an immune system without that flaw? To answer that question, we need to look at how our bodies maintain themselves.

Aging can be viewed simply as damage or deterioration that doesn't get repaired. We are unconsciously but constantly repairing ourselves at every level, from molecules to tissues to whole organs. In the same way, we spend money to repair our cars. Our bodies' self-repair mechanisms, like car repairs, fall into two categories: damage control and regular replacement.

For a car, damage control means things such as repairing a flat tire or replacing a smashed fender. For us, the most visible example of damage control is wound healing, which repairs damage to our skin. Some animals can achieve more spectacular damage control. Lizards regrow tails they have lost, starfish regrow severed limbs, and sea cucumbers can even regrow their intestines. At the invisible, molecular level, we have enzymes that recognize and fix damaged sites in our genetic material, DNA.

The other type of repair is regular replacement, also familiar to any car owner. We periodically change the oil, air filter, and other parts without waiting for the car to break down first. In the animal world, teeth are replaced on a scheduled basis. Humans go through two sets in their lifetime, elephants six sets, and sharks an indefinite number of sets. Lobsters and insects are among the creatures that regularly replace their external skeletons, or hard shells, by shedding them and growing new ones. Hair growth is another example of regular replacement. Hair keeps steadily growing, no matter how short we cut it.

Regular replacement also happens inside us. We constantly replace many of our cells: once every few days for the cells lining our intestines, for example, and once every four months for our red blood cells. To keep damaged molecules from building up in our bodies, our protein molecules are replaced, too. You may look the same in the mirror today as you did in a photo taken a month ago, but many of the individual molecules forming your body are different.

Much of an animal's body can be repaired if necessary, or is regularly replaced. The details of how much is repairable or replaceable vary from species to species, but there is nothing inevitable about the human limits. Since starfish can regrow amputated limbs, why can't we? To protect ourselves against arthritis, all we'd need is to regrow our joints periodically, like crabs. You might suppose that natural selection would favor the man or woman who didn't die at eighty but lived and produced babies until at least two hundred. So why can't we naturally repair or replace everything in our bodies?

The answer must have to do with the cost of repair. Think again about car repairs. Suppose you buy an expensive car that you expect to last for a long time, such as a Mercedes-Benz. It makes sense to invest in regular maintenance, which is cheaper than discarding your Mercedes and buying a new one every few years. But if you live in Port Moresby, New Guinea, the automobile accident capital of the world, any car is likely to be totaled within a year no matter how many oil changes and air filters you pay for. Many car owners there don't bother with maintenance—they use the money they save on maintenance to help pay for their next car.

In the same way, how much energy an animal "should" invest in biological repairs depends on the cost of the repairs, and how long the animal can expect to live with and without them. These considerations take us into the realm of evolutionary biology. Natural selection works to increase an organism's rate of leaving offspring that, in turn, survive to leave offspring of their own. Think of evolution as a strategy game. In evolutionary terms, the player whose strategy leaves the most descendants wins. This view helps us understand a number of biological problems, including life span.

The Problem of Life Span

If long life is good because it lets organisms leave more offspring, why don't plants and animals— and people—live longer? If speed and intelligence are good, why didn't we evolve to become even faster and smarter than we are now?

Natural selection acts on whole individuals, not on single parts or traits. It's you (not your big brain or fast legs) who does or doesn't survive and leave offspring. Increasing one part of an animal's body might be beneficial in one respect but harmful in some other ways. That larger part might not fit well with other parts of the same animal, or it might drain off energy from other parts.

Instead, natural selection tends to mold each trait to the degree that makes the most of the survival and reproductive success of the *whole animal*. Each trait doesn't increase to a possible maximum. Rather, all the traits meet at a point where they balance one another, with each trait neither too big nor too small. The whole animal is more successful than it would be if a given trait were bigger or smaller.

Once again, we can see how this principle works if we look at a complex piece of machinery, such as a car. Engineers can't tinker with single parts in isolation from the rest of the machine, because each part costs money, space, and weight that could have gone into something else. Engineers have to ask what *combination* of parts will make the machine most effective.

In a way, evolution is like an engineer. It can't tinker with single traits in isolation from the rest of an animal, because every organ, enzyme, or piece of DNA consumes energy and space that might have gone into something else. Instead, natural selection favors the combination of traits that gives the animal the greatest reproductive success. Both engineers and evolutionary biologists must consider the trade-offs involved in increasing anything. They must weigh the costs as well as the benefits the change would bring.

THE LESSON OF THE BATTLE CRUISERS

FOR AN EXAMPLE OF A SPECIES IN WHICH one trait became huge, leading to the species' extinction, consider the British battle cruiser. Before and during World War I (1914–1918), the British navy launched thirteen of these warships. They were designed to be as large as battleships, with as many big guns as a battleship, but much faster. By maximizing speed and firepower, the battle cruisers immediately caught the public's imagination and became a propaganda sensation.

But . . . if you take a 28,000-ton battleship, keep the weight of the big guns almost the same, and greatly increase the size of the engines for greater speed, all while keeping the overall weight of the vessel at 28,000 tons, you have to skimp on some of the other parts.

The battle cruisers skimped especially on the weight of their armor, but also on the weight of their smaller guns, internal compartments, and antiaircraft defense.

The result of this unbalanced design was inevitable. In 1916 the battle cruisers HMS *Indefatigable*, *Queen Mary*, and *Invincible* all blew up almost as soon as they were hit by German shells in a single battle. HMS *Hood* blew up in 1941, eight minutes after entering battle with the German battleship *Bismarck*. A few days after the Japanese attack on Pearl Harbor in 1941, HMS *Repulse* was sunk by Japanese bombers, becoming the first large warship to be destroyed from the air while in combat at sea. Faced with this clear evidence that spectacularly beefing up some parts doesn't make a well-balanced whole, the British navy let its program of building battle cruisers go extinct.

(*above*)
The HMS *Queen Mary* after it was hit by German shells in WWI in 1916.

Evolution and Aging

Our life cycles have many features that seem to limit, not maximize, our ability to produce offspring. Growing old and dying is one example. Others include our late puberty, our nine-month-long pregnancies, our single births, and the female menopause (the point in a woman's life when she stops being able to bear children). Why wouldn't natural selection favor a woman who entered puberty at five, completed a full pregnancy in three weeks, always bore five or more children, never entered menopause, and lived to two hundred, leaving behind hundreds of offspring?

Asking that question pretends that evolution can change our bodies one piece at a time, and it ignores the hidden costs. Humans could not reduce the length of pregnancy to three weeks, for example, without changing other things about ourselves and our babies. Remember that we have only a limited amount of energy available to us. Even people doing hard work, such as lumberjacks or marathon runners, can turn only about six thousand calories a day into energy. If our goal is to produce as many babies as possible, how would we divide those calories between rearing babies and repairing ourselves to live longer?

At one extreme, if we put all our energy into babies and none into biological repair, our bodies would age and disintegrate before we could rear our first baby. At the other extreme, if we spent all our energy on keeping our bodies functioning well, we might live a long time but we would have no energy for the exhausting business of making and rearing babies.

What natural selection must do is adjust the amounts of energy a species spends on repair and reproduction to arrive at the maximum number of offspring averaged over a lifetime. The result is a balance between life span and the reproductive traits of the life cycle. That balance varies from one animal species to another.

A two-month-old mouse, for example, can make baby mice, while it takes at least a dozen years, often longer, for a human to become physically capable of reproduction. Even a well-fed and cared-for mouse, though, is lucky to reach its second birthday. A well-fed and cared-for human is unlucky not to reach his or her seventy-second.

Animals like us, who start having offspring after a number of years, must devote a lot of energy to self-repair so that we live long enough to reach reproductive age. As a result, we age far more slowly than mice, probably because we repair our bodies much more effectively. (Much of our maintenance and self-repair, remember, goes into the invisible, scheduled replacement of our cells.) A human who invested no more energy into self-repair than a mouse would die long before reaching puberty.

IS THERE A CAUSE OF AGING?

RESEARCHERS IN GERONTOLOGY, THE STUDY
of aging, focus on the physiological aspects of
age and death. They search for a Cause of Aging,
or at most a few causes. Evolutionary biology,
though, suggests that they will not succeed.
There should not be a single cause of aging, or
even a few. Instead, natural selection should act
to match the rates of aging in all our systems,
so that getting older and dying involves many
changes happening at the same time.

There's no point in doing expensive
maintenance on one part of the body if other
parts are deteriorating faster because so
much energy goes into that maintenance.
There's also no point in allowing a few parts
or systems to deteriorate long before the
rest if spending energy to repair just those
few systems would bring a big increase in

life expectancy. Natural selection doesn't make pointless mistakes. The best strategy is to repair all parts at whatever rates allow everything finally to collapse all at once.

I believe that the evolutionary ideal of total collapse describes the fates of our bodies better than the physiologists' long-sought single Cause of Aging. Most people as they age experience tooth wear or loss, decreases in muscle strength, and significant losses in hearing, vision, smell, and taste. Weakening of the heart, hardening of the arteries, brittleness of bones, decrease in kidney function, lowered

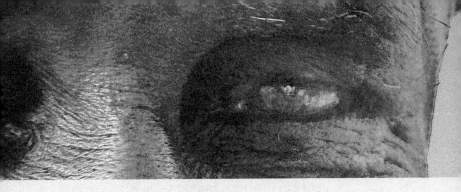

resistance of the immune system, and loss of
memory are also common symptoms of aging.
Evolution does seem to have arranged things
so that all our systems deteriorate.

From a practical viewpoint, this is
disappointing. If there were one single or
dominant cause of aging, curing that cause would
give us a fountain of youth. Natural selection,
though, would not permit us to deteriorate
through a single mechanism with a simple cure.
Perhaps that's just as well. What would the world
be like if we all lived for centuries? What use
would we make of our extra time?

Life after Reproduction

For a key example of how evolution can explain some facts about aging, let's examine a unique feature of the human lifestyle, which is that we survive past reproductive age. Passing one's genes to the next generation is what drives evolution. Animals of other species rarely live on after they stop reproducing. Nature programs death to happen when fertility ends, because there's no evolutionary benefit in keeping a body in good repair when it is longer making babies.

So why are human women programmed to live for decades after menopause, and why are human men programmed to live to an age when most of them are no longer busy fathering babies?

The answer lies in human parental care. In the human species, the intense phase of parental care is unusually long: nearly two decades. Even older people whose own children have reached adulthood are important to those children. By helping to care for their grandchildren and other youngsters, they contribute to survival—not just of their own children and grandchildren but of their whole tribe. Especially in the days before writing, older people were carriers of essential knowledge. For this reason, nature has programmed us to keep our bodies in reasonable repair at relatively advanced ages, even after women reach menopause and can no longer bear children.

But why did natural selection program female menopause into us in the first place? Most mammals, including human males and gorillas and chimpanzees of both sexes, merely experience a gradual decline and eventual end of fertility as they grow older. Only human females experience the abrupt shutdown of fertility that is menopause. Wouldn't natural selection favor the woman who remained fertile until the bitter end?

Human female menopause probably resulted from two other uniquely human characteristics. One is the exceptional danger that childbirth poses to the mother. Compared with other species, human babies are enormous relative to their mothers' size. Childbirth can be a difficult, even dangerous, matter. Before modern medical care, women often died while giving birth, and this still happens today, although it has become much rarer than it used to be. Among other primates, it has always been rare for mothers to die in childbirth.

The other characteristic is the danger that a mother's death poses to her children, who are extremely dependent on her for care. Because children need parental care for a long time, even after they are no longer nursing, the death of a hunter-gatherer mother would probably have meant that her children likely died, too. This would have remained true up to a later age in childhood than for any other species of primate.

A hunter-gatherer mother with several children, then, risked the lives of those children every time she gave birth to a new baby. As each of her children grew older, her investment in that child's care grew larger. At the same time, her own risk of dying in childbirth also increased as she got older. This meant that the danger to her existing children got worse and worse with each new pregnancy. When you already have three living children still dependent on you, having a fourth runs the risk of leaving those three motherless.

Those worsening odds probably led to menopause through natural selection. Shutting down female fertility protects a mother's investment in the children she has already borne. But because childbirth carries no risk of death for fathers, men did not evolve menopause. Like aging, menopause is a feature of our life cycle that is hard to understand without the context of evolution. It's even possible that menopause evolved only within the past sixty thousand years, when Cro-Magnons and other anatomically modern humans began regularly living to the age of sixty and beyond.

The longer life span of modern humans rests not only on cultural adaptations, such as tools for getting food or fighting predators, but also on the biological adaptations of menopause and increased investment in self-repair. Whether those biological adaptations developed at the time of the Great Leap Forward or earlier, they rank among the life history changes that made the third chimpanzee human.

Hawaiian schoolchildren around 1914. At that time young people like these, from many ethnic backgrounds, were turning the pidgin language of their plantation-worker parents into a fully functioning creole language.

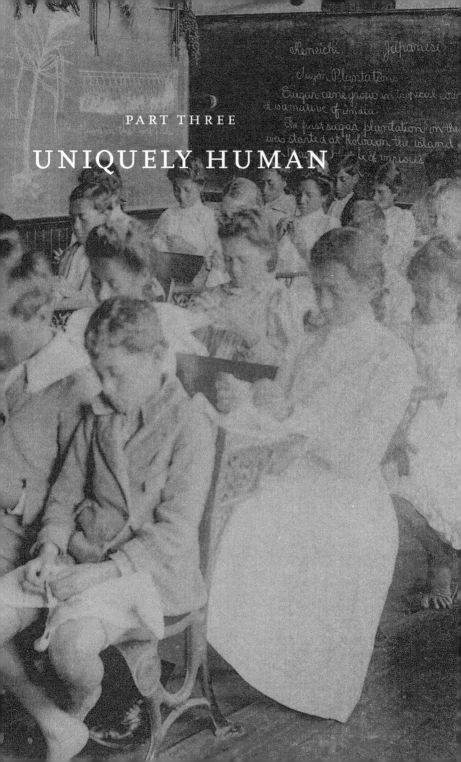

PART THREE

UNIQUELY HUMAN

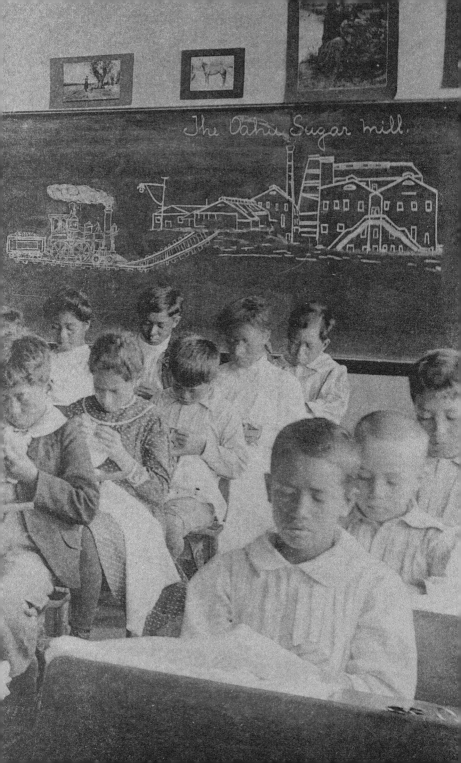

BIOLOGY IS THE BASIS FOR SOME OF OUR uniquely human traits, as we saw in parts 1 and 2. Our large brains and the fact that we walk upright are determined by our genes. So are some features of our bodies and life cycles.

If those were our only unique traits, we wouldn't stand out among animals. Ostriches walk on two legs. Some other animals have big brains relative to the size of their bodies. Seabirds live in large colonies the way we do, and tortoises, like humans, have long life spans. Our uniqueness lies in the cultural traits that rest on our genetic foundations. These cultural traits— spoken language, art, tool-based technology, and agriculture—give us our power.

If we stopped there, we'd have a one-sided, positive view of our uniqueness. Archaeology shows that our invention of agriculture was a mixed blessing that has seriously harmed many people while benefiting others. And we have other, darker traits. One is chemical abuse, our tendency to consume things, such as toxic drugs, that are harmful to us. At least that doesn't threaten our survival as a species. Two of our other cultural practices—to be discussed in parts 4 and 5—do threaten our survival. One is genocide, the killing of whole groups of people. The other is the mass extermination of other species, which often goes along with the destruction of the environment, our own habitat. These traits make us uncomfortable. Are they occasional, unnatural outbreaks, or are they features as basic to humanity as the traits we're proudest of?

None of these human traits, good or bad, could have arisen from nothing. For each of them, we need to ask: What behavior in the animal world might have given rise to this human trait? Can we trace the appearance and evolution of this trait in our family tree? The next four chapters consider these questions for traits that are noble, two-edged, or only mildly destructive: language, art, agriculture, and chemical abuse. I'll end this part by examining the search for intelligent life on other planets, and by showing what we can learn about life in the universe from studies of woodpecker evolution right here on earth.

CHAPTER 6

THE MYSTERY OF LANGUAGE

THE ORIGIN OF LANGUAGE IS THE MOST
important mystery in how we became uniquely
human. Language lets us communicate
with each other far more precisely than any
animals can do. It lets us make group plans,
teach one another, and learn from what people
have experienced in other places or in the
past. This is why I think that the Great Leap
Forward—the stage in human history when
our ability to invent new ways of doing things
finally appeared—was made possible by the
development of spoken language as we know it.

The Lack of a Time Machine
Animals communicate, but between human

language and the sounds made by any animal lies a gulf that doesn't seem crossable. How was it crossed? We evolved from animals that lacked human speech, so our language must have evolved over time, along with other human features such as the shape of our skulls or our ability to make tools and art.

Unfortunately, the origins of language are harder to trace than the origins of our skulls, tools, or art. The spoken word vanishes in an instant. I often dream of a time machine that would let me place tape recorders in the camps of our ancient ancestors. Perhaps I'd discover that australopithecines, the African man-apes of millions of years ago, uttered grunts not too different from those of chimpanzees. Maybe *Homo erectus* used recognizable single words and then, after a million years or so, progressed to two-word sentences. Before the Great Leap Forward, *Homo sapiens* may have gotten as far as longer strings of words, but without much grammar, and the full range of modern speech arrived only with the Leap.

With no prospects of ever getting that time machine, how can we hope to trace speech origins? Two fast-growing bodies of knowledge may let us start to build bridges across that gulf between animal sounds and human language.

First, we'll look at the animal side of the language bridge. This approach draws on new studies of the vocalizations of wild animal: the cries, calls, grunts, and other sounds that animals use to communicate among themselves. We are beginning to sense how far animals have come toward inventing their own languages.

Then we'll examine the human side of the bridge. All existing human languages seem infinitely more advanced than animal sounds. Yet one set of human languages may hold clues to some early stages in the development of language.

Listening to Vervets

Birds sing. Dogs bark. Many of us have a good chance of hearing some calling animal on most days of our lives. Our understanding of animal sounds exploded when we developed new tools and techniques, such as high-quality recorders to capture animal sounds in the wild, electronic software to analyze subtle variations in the sounds, and methods of broadcasting calls back to animals to see how they'd react. Animal vocal communication, scientists are discovering, is much more language-like than anyone would have guessed half a century ago.

The most sophisticated "animal language" yet

studied is that of the vervet, a monkey about the size of a cat that is common in Africa. Wild vervets are equally at home in trees and on the ground of the savanna or the rain forest. Like other animals, they regularly face situations in which efficient communication would help them to survive.

About three-quarters of wild vervet deaths are caused by predators. If you're a vervet, it's essential to know the difference between a martial eagle, one of the leading killers of vervets, and a white-backed vulture, a bird of about the same size as the eagle but that eats dead things and is no danger to live monkeys. When an eagle appears, you must take defensive measures, and tell your relatives. If you fail to recognize the eagle, you die. If you fail to tell your relatives, they die, carrying some of your genes with them. If you think it's an eagle when it's really a vulture, you waste time running down from the treetop while other vervets are safely up there gathering food.

Besides the problem of predators, vervets have complex social relationships with one another. They live in groups and compete for territory with other groups. If you're a vervet, you need to know the difference between a monkey intruding from another group, an unrelated member of your

(*left*)
A female vervet monkey with young. Mother vervets give more alarm calls—warnings against leopards and other predators—when they are with their own offspring than when they are with other monkeys.

own group who is likely to steal your food, and a close relative who will support you. If you get into trouble, you need to be able to tell your relatives that *you* are in trouble, not some other monkey. It would also be useful to share news about where to find edible fruits and seeds.

Studies of vervet behavior have revealed that these monkeys communicate specific information about predators. When vervets encounter a leopard or other large wild cat, male monkeys give a loud series of barks, females give a high-pitched chirp, and all monkeys within earshot may run up a tree. The sight of an eagle overhead causes vervets to give a short, two-syllable cough, which causes other monkeys to look up into the air or run into a bush. And a monkey who spots a python or other dangerous snake gives a "chuttering" call, which leads other monkeys to stand on their hind legs and look down for the snake.

These three calls by no means make up a vervet's entire vocabulary. Other, fainter alarm calls appear to be triggered by baboons, jackals and hyenas, and humans. Vervets also utter gruntlike calls when interacting with one another. Even to scientists who have spent years studying vervets, the grunts all sound the same. Electronic measuring, though, showed differences in the grunts when monkeys interact with those higher or lower than themselves in their troop's pecking order, or when they watch another monkey, or when they see a rival troop.

How do we know the vervet's calls are meant to communicate with other monkeys? Could they be simply automatic expressions of fear or alarm, the way a human might shriek with terror when watching a scary movie, even if no one else is around to hear? There are several reasons to think that vervets are deliberately communicating with one another.

One piece of evidence is that a solitary vervet was observed being chased by a leopard for nearly an hour but remained silent through the whole ordeal. There were no other monkeys around, so it had no need to communicate. Another bit of evidence is that mother vervets give more alarm calls when they are with their offspring than when they are with unrelated monkeys. Finally, when two troops are fighting, a vervet in the losing troop may give the "leopard call" even though there is no leopard. The call sends all the monkeys scrambling into the trees. It is a deceptive "time out" that breaks up the fight. In addition, young vervets appear to learn how to utter and respond to sounds, just as human infants do. A young vervet's "pronunciation" gets better as it gets older, and so does its reaction to the various calls.

Are vervets sounds "words" or "sentences"? Does the "leopard call" mean "leopard" or does it mean "There goes a leopard" or "Watch out for that leopard!" or "Let's run up a tree to get away from that leopard!"? It may be a combination of all of them. I was excited when my one-year-old son, Max, said, "Juice." What I proudly saw as one of his first words, though, he meant as "Give me some juice!" Only at a later age did he add the syllables that show the difference between sentences and pure words. Vervets show no sign of having reached that stage.

Apes That "Speak"

Apes are more closely related to us than monkeys are, and they also make sounds. Vocal communication by wild chimps and other apes, however, is much harder to study than communication by wild vervets, because apes' territories are much larger. The study of captive apes cannot reproduce all the qualities of an ape community in the wild. For this reason we are just beginning to learn about how wild apes use their natural "languages." But through a different approach we have learned something about apes' ability to communicate.

Several groups of scientists have spent years training captive gorillas, common chimpanzees, and bonobos to understand and use artificial languages. The scientists have used plastic pieces of different sizes and colors as symbols to represent words. They have also used hand signs based on the signs deaf people use, and keyboards with each key bearing a symbol. Through these methods, apes have learned the meanings of as many as several hundred symbols. At least one captive bonobo, or pygmy chimp, has been found to understand a good deal of spoken English—but not to speak it. These studies show that apes have the mental ability to master large vocabularies.

The anatomy of apes' vocal tracts keeps them from producing as many vowels and consonants as we can utter. For this reason the vocabulary of wild apes is unlikely to be anywhere near as large as our own. Still, I expect wild chimp and gorilla vocabularies to be larger than vervet vocabularies. Apes might use several dozen "words," possibly including names for individual animals. In this exciting field in which new knowledge is being rapidly gained, we should keep an open mind on the size of the vocabulary gap between apes and humans.

WHO BIT WHOM?

HUMANS DON'T JUST HAVE VOCABULARIES of thousands of words with different meanings. We also combine those words, and change their forms, according to rules of grammar, including syntax, which means the rules of word order. Grammar lets us build a potentially unlimited number of sentences from a limited number of words.

To appreciate the importance of syntax, think about the following two sentences. They have the same words but different word orders.

"Your hungry dog bit my old mother's leg."

"My hungry mother bit your old dog's leg."

If human language did not involve grammatical rules, these two sentences would have exactly the same meaning. Most linguists (people who study language and how it is structured) would not consider an animal's sounds to be language, no matter how large its vocabulary, unless it also had grammatical rules.

Do any animals have grammar? No hint of syntax has been discovered in vervet calls so far. Capuchin monkeys and gibbons do have calls they use only in certain combinations or sequences, but we have not yet figured out what this means. Some recent findings suggest that finches and possibly other birds may use a form of syntax in their calls, but more research is needed.

Wild chimpanzees are the animals most likely to use grammar. I doubt, though, that anyone expects them to have evolved a grammar even remotely as complex as human grammar, which has prepositions; verb tenses to signal past, present, and future; and other structures. For now, it is an open question whether any animal has evolved syntax.

The Human Side of the Language Bridge

The gulf between animal and human communication is surely large, but scientists are gaining an understanding of how that gulf has been bridged from the animal side. Now let's trace the bridge from the human side. We have already discovered complex animal "languages." Do any truly primitive human languages still exist?

To help us recognize what a primitive language might be like, let's look at how normal human language differs from vervet vocalizations. One difference is that human languages have grammar, rules that govern how words are used to make sentences. A second difference is that vervet vocalizations stand for things that can be seen or actions that can be taken, such as "eagle" or "watch out for the eagle!" But up to half the words in human speech—words such as *and, because,* and *should*—do not refer to anything you can see or do.

A third difference is that human languages have a hierarchical structure. This means that they consist of different levels: sounds, syllables, words, phrases, sentences. Each level is built on the level below it, and is bigger than that level. On the bottom level, we make a few dozen sounds. At the next level, these sounds combine into many different syllables. These syllables, in turn, combine to make thousands of words, which we string into phrases according to the rules of grammar. Phrases then interlock to make a huge, potentially infinite, number of sentences.

The oldest known written languages date from about five thousand years ago. They were as complex as the languages of today, which means that human language must have reached its modern level of complexity long before that. Are there any peoples existing today with simple languages that might show us the early stages of language evolution?

The answer is no. Some hunter-gatherers or other preindustrial groups in the modern world still use Stone Age tools, or did until recently, but their spoken languages are as modern and complex as ours, or as the written languages of fifty centuries ago. To investigate human language origins, we need a different approach.

How New Languages Are Born

One approach is to ask: Would people who never hear a fully evolved modern language invent a primitive language of their own?

In fact, children who grow up alone, away from other people, do not invent or discover a language of their own. But dozens of times in the modern world, whole populations of children have grown up hearing the adults around them speaking a drastically simplified language, similar to what children themselves speak around the age of two. These crude languages are called pidgins. Children who grow up hearing pidgin evolve their own language, far more advanced than vervet communications, more complex than pidgin, but still simpler than normal human languages. These second-generation invented languages are called creoles.

Why would whole populations of adults talk like two-year-olds? Pidgins form when two groups who speak different languages need to communicate with each other—for example, when people from one part of the world start to colonize or trade in another territory. Within their own group, people speak their own native language. To communicate with people from the other group, they use pidgin. This is what happened when English-speaking traders and sailors arrived in the island of New Guinea in the early nineteenth century.

(*left*)
In the creole language of Guadeloupe, an island in the Caribbean, this sign reads, "Slow down, children are playing here!"

At that time, the people of New Guinea spoke about seven hundred different languages. For both English speakers and the people of New Guinea to communicate across groups, there had to be a common, or shared, language that anyone could use. A pidgin developed, made up of simple words. In time that crude pidgin evolved into a more advanced creole that is now called Neo-Melanesian. Today Neo-Melanesian serves New Guinea not only as the language of much conversation but also of many schools, newspapers, and media and government activities.

How does a pidgin become a creole? Let's start with a look at how a pidgin works. Compared with normal languages, pidgins are poor in sounds, vocabulary, and syntax. An early-stage pidgin is mostly nouns, verbs, and adjectives. As for grammar, conversation usually consists of short strings of words, with few or no rules about word order or other variations. A pidgin is a kind of language free-for-all, with different speakers using it in different ways.

If adults keep using their native languages most of the time, speaking pidgin only occasionally when necessary, the pidgin stays at the same crude level. But if a whole generation begins to use pidgin as its native language—for all social purposes, not just for work or trade—the pidgin will evolve into a creole, with a larger vocabulary and much more complex grammar.

Even without an authority to set out the specific rules of this new grammar, the pidgin will become larger and more definite, until it is a creole. And although a creole is simpler than a normal language, it can express just about any thought that a normal language can express, while it is a struggle to say anything even slightly complex in a pidgin.

HAWAIIAN CHILDREN CREATE A LANGUAGE

IN THE LATE NINETEENTH CENTURY,
American owners of Hawaiian sugarcane plantations
brought in workers from China, the Philippines,
Japan, Korea, Portugal, and Puerto Rico. Amid the
chaos of languages, a pidgin based on English arose.
Immigrant workers kept speaking their own native
languages within their groups, while using the pidgin
to communicate with people from other groups.

Here's an example of pidgin as it was spoken by
people who came to Hawaii around 1900: "Me cape
buy, me check make." *Cape*, pronounced "kah-pee,"
was the pidgin word for "coffee." This example of a
pidgin sentence could mean two very different things.
It could mean either "He bought my coffee, he made
me out a check," *or* "I bought coffee, I made him out
a check." The people having the conversation would
have to figure out the meaning depending on what
else was being said or done at the time.

Hawaiian workers did not improve on the pidgin they used, even though it was a very limited form of communication. That was a problem for the immigrants' children born in Hawaii. Some children heard pidgin at home because their parents came from different ethnic groups. Even if both parents spoke the same native language at home, kids could not use that home language to communicate with children or adults from other groups. And social barriers prevented workers' children from mixing with the plantation owners and, thereby, learning English.

The kids' solution was to turn the limited plantation pidgin into a full-fledged creole within a single generation. This process was recorded by a researcher who interviewed working-class Hawaiians in the 1970s. Because older people still spoke the form of language they had heard around them and learned in their youth, the researcher was able to trace steps in the transition

The Oahu Sugar Mill.

from pidgin to creole. He found that creolization started around 1900 and was complete by 1920.

Creole allowed young Hawaiians to express more complicated thoughts, using sentences that had a single, definite meaning. For example, "Da firs japani came ran away from japan come" meant "The first Japanese who arrived ran away from Japan to here." And "One day had pleny dis mountain fish come down," meant "One day there were a lot of these fish from the mountains that came down [the river]."

Hawaiian children created creole from pidgin as they learned to speak. While they communicated among themselves, grammar evolved. The result was something different from English and also different from the languages of all the worker groups. The children had invented a language.

The Language Blueprint

The birth of a pidgin that grows into a creole is a natural experiment in language evolution. It has unfolded dozens of times in the modern world, from South America through Africa to the Pacific islands, from at least the seventeenth century to the twentieth.

The outcomes of all these language experiments are remarkably similar. Most creoles share certain features, such as putting a sentence's subject, verb, and object in that order. It is as if you drew a dozen cards fifty times from well-shuffled decks and almost always ended up with no hearts or diamonds, but with one queen, a jack, and two aces. How could creoles that evolved in so many different places and times be so similar?

I think the likeliest explanation is one that some language researchers have suggested. They think that humans share a genetic blueprint for learning language during childhood. In other words, much of language's structure is hardwired, or programmed, into us by our genes. A hardwired language structure might produce the patterns that we see again and again in creole grammars. And on that foundation, over time, people could have built the great variety of the world's fully developed languages.

Now let's pull together animal and human studies to try to form a picture of how our ancestors progressed from grunts to Shakespeare's sonnets. The first stage is animal calls that carry specific meanings, such as those of vervets. The single words of young human toddlers represent the next stage—not just a grunt, but a word assembled from a set of vowels and consonants that can also be used to make many other words.

The next step is represented by two-year-old children. In all human societies, two-year-olds move spontaneously from one-word utterances to strings of two words, and then more. But these utterances are still just word strings with little grammar, and the words are nouns, verbs, and adjectives. Two-year-olds' word strings are like the first stages of pidgins, or like the strings of words made by captive apes who have learned how to use symbols.

From pidgins to creoles, or from the word strings of two-year-olds to the complete sentences of four-year-olds, is a giant step. This step adds elements of grammar, such as prefixes, suffixes, and word order. It adds words that do not refer to things in the real world but that, instead, have grammatical functions, such as *and, or, before*, and *if*. In this stage, words are arranged into phrases and sentences. Perhaps this giant step is what triggered the Great Leap Forward.

Animal and human communication once seemed to be separated by an unbridgeable gulf. Now we have identified parts of bridges starting from the opposite shores, and some stepping-stones spaced across the gulf. We are beginning to understand how language, the most unique and important human characteristic, arose from our origins in the animal world.

CHAPTER 7

ANIMAL ORIGINS OF ART

SIRI'S DRAWINGS WON PRAISE AS SOON AS other artists saw them. Willem de Kooning, a famous painter, said, "They had a kind of flair and decisiveness and originality." Jerome Witkin, an art expert and professor, said, "This drawing indicates a grasp of the essential mark that makes the emotion."

Who was Siri, this remarkable new artist? Witkin guessed from her drawings that she was female and interested in Asian decorative lettering. What he did not know was that she was eight feet tall and weighed four tons. Siri was an Asian elephant who drew by holding a pencil in her trunk.

Actually, Siri wasn't extraordinary by elephant standards. Wild elephants often use their trunks to make drawing motions in the dust. Captive

(*left*)
Congo the chimpanzee finishes a painting. Although he and other animals have produced artwork that has impressed—and sometimes fooled—art critics, these animal artists lived in captivity. Wild chimpanzees have not yet been seen making art, although their closest relatives take great pride in their artistic creations.

elephants often scratch marks on the ground using a stick or stone. A captive elephant named Carol made paintings that sold for hundreds of dollars and ended up on the walls of many doctors' and lawyers' offices.

Supposedly, art is the noblest unique human trait. It sets us apart from animals at least as much as language does. Language, however, serves a useful purpose, but art has no obvious function. Its origins are considered a sublime mystery.

There are huge differences between Siri's art and the work of human artists. (For one thing, Siri wasn't trying to communicate her message to other elephants.) Still, it's a similar physical activity that creates products that even experts can't tell from human artistic productions. And the artlike activities of animals such as elephants may help us understand how human art originally functioned.

What Is Art?

If we're going to claim that true art is unique to humans, what makes it different from animal productions that may seem similar? How is our music different from birdsong? People have made three claims about how human art is different from anything animals do.

First, art has no utilitarian purpose—in other words, it is not useful. To a biologist, "useful" means that it helps us to survive or to pass on our genes to offspring. The claim is that human art does not fulfill those functions. Birdsong, in contrast, helps birds attract mates and defend territory, and this in turn lets them pass their genes to the next generation.

Second, art is just for aesthetic pleasure, or the appreciation of beauty. A dictionary defines art as "the making or doing of things that have form or beauty." While we can't ask mockingbirds or nightingales if they enjoy the form and beauty of their songs, it's significant that they sing mainly during the breeding season. This strongly suggests that they're singing not for aesthetic pleasure but to court their mates and defend their nesting territories.

Third, art is taught and learned, not something passed down to us in our genes. Each human group has its own distinctive art style. Knowledge of how to make and enjoy that style is learned, not inherited. For example, it's easy to tell apart traditional songs sung in Tokyo and

Paris. But those differences aren't hardwired into our genes. French and Japanese people can learn each other's songs. Many species of birds, in contrast, inherit the knowledge of how to make and respond to the particular song of their species. Each of those birds would produce the right song even if it never heard it, or heard only the songs of other species.

Keeping these claims about human art in mind, let's now examine some more examples of animal art.

Ape Artists

Human art may seem far removed from Siri's drawings and Carol's paintings. After all, elephants aren't even closely related to us in evolutionary terms. What about art produced by our primate relatives?

Captive chimpanzees, gorillas, orangutans, and even monkeys have produced art, either by painting with a finger or a brush, or by using pencil, chalk, or crayons. A chimp named Congo did up to thirty-three paintings in one day. He must have done them for his own satisfaction, because he did not show his work to other chimps and threw a tantrum when his brush was taken away. Congo and another chimp, Betsy, were honored by a show of their work in London in 1957, and Congo had another show the following year.

Almost all the paintings at those chimp shows were sold (to human buyers). Plenty of human artists can't make that boast. Still other ape paintings were sneaked into exhibits of work made by human artists. Art critics, with no idea that certain paintings had been made by apes, enthusiastically praised those works.

Child psychologists were given paintings made by chimpanzees at the Baltimore Zoo and asked to diagnose the painters' mental problems—without being told that the painters were chimps. The psychologists guessed that a painting by a three-year-old male chimp had been made by an aggressive seven- or eight-year-old boy. They also guessed that two paintings by a one-year-old female chimp were by two different, but disturbed, ten-year-old girls. The psychologists got the gender of each artist right. They were only wrong about the species.

These paintings by our closest relatives start to blur the line between human art and animal activities. Like human paintings, the ape paintings served no clear purpose. They were produced just for satisfaction. There is, though, a problem with claiming a parallel between ape art and human art. Ape painting is just an unnatural activity of captive animals. It does not occur in the wild.

You could argue that because ape painting is not a natural behavior, it cannot shed light on the possible animal origins of art. So let's turn now to a natural behavior, the activity of bowerbirds. These birds create bowers, the most elaborate structures built and decorated by any animal species other than humans.

THE OLDEST ART

WE HUMANS MANAGED TO DO WITHOUT ART for the first 6,960,000 years of the 7 million or so years since we separated from chimps. Our earliest art forms may have been wood carving and body painting, but we wouldn't know this today, because those art forms could not have been preserved in the fossil record. The first preserved hints of human art are some flower remains around Neanderthal skeletons (possible grave decorations), and some scratches on bones at Neanderthal campsites. We don't know whether Neanderthals deliberately scattered those flowers or scratched those bones. They may be art, but they may simply be accidents.

Our first definite evidence for art comes from the Cro-Magnon people of western Europe about sixty thousand years ago. Many examples survive, including statues, necklaces, and flutes and other musical instruments. Most famous are the many paintings—mostly of animals, some now extinct—that these humans left on cave walls in France and Spain.

Beauty and the Bird

If I hadn't already heard of bowers, I'd have thought the first one I saw was man-made, as nineteenth-century explorers did.

I had set out that morning from a New Guinea village of circular huts, neat rows of flowers, and people wearing decorative beads. Suddenly, in the jungle, I came across a beautifully woven circular hut eight feet around and four feet high, with a doorway large enough for a child to enter.

In front of the hut was a lawn of green moss, clean except for hundreds of natural objects that had obviously been placed there as decorations. These were mainly flowers, fruits, and leaves, with some fungi and butterfly wings. Objects of similar colors were grouped together—red fruits next to red leaves, for example. The largest decorations were a tall pile of black fungi facing the door and a pile of orange fungi a few yards away. All the blue objects had been placed inside the hut.

That hut was not a child's playground. It had been built and decorated by a bird about the size of a jay—a bowerbird. These birds are found only in New Guinea and Australia. There are eighteen species, and in each species the male

(*left*)
Bowerbirds' complex creations are beautiful, but bower building evolved and lasted because it serves a purpose. By building an excellent bower, a male bird shows females that he has the right stuff to be a good mate.

birds build bowers for one purpose: to seduce females. Building the bower is the male's contribution to family life. Once he has mated with a female, she will build a nest and rear their young, while he tries to mate with as many other females as he can.

Females, often in groups, cruise around the bowers in their vicinity and inspect them all before choosing a mate. They select their mate by the quality of his bower, the number of its decorations, and how well it fits the local rules of bower building, which vary from place to place. Some populations of bowerbirds prefer blue decorations, others red or green or gray, while some build, in place of a hut, one or two towers, a two-walled avenue, or a four-walled box. There are populations that paint their bowers with crushed leaves or with oils from their bodies.

These local differences appear not to be hardwired into the birds' genes. Instead, as young birds grow up, they watch older ones. In this way, male bowerbirds learn the locally correct way to decorate. Females learn the same rules, to help them pick their mates.

But what good does it do a female bowerbird to pick the guy who decorated his bower with the blue fruit?

Animals don't have time to produce ten offspring with ten different mates to find out which mate produces the greatest number of surviving offspring. Instead, they use shortcuts. They rely on mating signals, such as songs, or ritual displays of markings or feathers—or bowers. Experts in animal behavior are hotly debating why those mating signals are a sign of good genes, or even *if* they are a sign of good genes.

Think, though, about what it means when a female bowerbird finds a male with a good bower. She knows he is strong, because his bower weighs hundreds of times his own weight and he had to drag some heavy decorations for dozens of yards. She knows he has the mechanical skill to weave hundreds of sticks into a hut, towers, or walls. He must have a good brain, to carry out this complex task. He must have good vision and memory, to search out the necessary decorations in the jungle. And he must be dominant over other males. Male bowerbirds spend much of their time trying to wreck or steal from one another's bowers. Only the winners end up with undamaged, well-decorated bowers.

Bower building is a well-rounded test of a male bird's genes. It's as if women put each of their suitors through a weight-lifting contest, a sewing contest, a chess tournament, an eye test, and a boxing match before choosing the winner as her mate.

How did bowerbirds evolve to use art so cleverly for such important purposes? Most birds woo females by advertising their colorful bodies, their songs, or their offerings of food to hint at good genes. Male birds of paradise in New Guinea go further by clearing patches of forest floor to show off their fancy plumage. One bird of paradise species goes further still. Males decorate their cleared areas with items useful to a nesting female, such as pieces of snakeskin to line her nest, or fruit to eat. The bowerbirds have taken the next step. In the course of bowerbird evolution, they learned that decorative objects don't have to be useful. Even useless decorations can signal good genes if those decorations were difficult to get and keep.

Art Serves a Purpose

With bowerbirds in mind, let's look again at those three claims that supposedly set human art apart from animal activities. They are: art is not useful, art is made for aesthetic pleasure alone, and art is learned, not inborn.

Both bower styles and our art styles are learned rather than inherited, which takes care of the third claim. As for aesthetic pleasure, no answer is possible. We can't ask bowerbirds if they get pleasure out of making or looking at bowers. That leaves only the idea that true art has no use in the biological sense. That is definitely untrue of bower art, which has the sexual function of helping males get mates. Does human art also serve any biological functions? Does it help us to survive and pass on our genes?

Art—including dance, music, and poetry— often serves a seductive purpose, or is a beginning to romantic attachment or even sexual activity. This is a direct benefit, but art also brings indirect benefits to its owner. Art is a quick indicator of status, which in human *and* animal societies is a key to acquiring food, land, and mates. Art is often viewed as a sign of talent, money, or both. Some artists can also turn their art into food. Not only do successful individual artists make money by selling their art, but whole societies have supported themselves by making art for trade with other groups that produce food. The Siassi islanders, for example, lived off the coast of New Guinea on tiny islets with little room for gardens. They survived by carving beautiful bowls that other tribes paid for with food.

Art not only brings benefits to individuals but helps define human groups. People have always formed competing groups. Within each group, individuals depend on the help and protection of the other members of the group. That means that for a man or woman in a group to live long enough to marry, have children, and pass on his or her genes, the group must survive. A group is more likely to survive if it sticks together and remains unified. Cohesion, the group's ability to stick together, depends on its distinctive culture, which includes language, religion, and art. In other words, art is one of the things that contribute to a group's, and an individual's, identity.

What about people who simply enjoy art, without using it to get money or mates? Isn't private satisfaction a main reason for our art, just as it was for Siri the elephant and Congo the chimp? Of course. Art-making behavior may have started because it was useful, but animals that have leisure time—once they have brought their survival problems under control—can expand behaviors far beyond their original role.

If human art did evolve because it brought useful benefits to individuals and groups, it later came to serve other purposes. Those additional purposes include representing information (a possible explanation of the Cro-Magnon paintings of game animals), relieving boredom (a real problem for captive elephants and other animals), channeling nervous energy (a problem for us as well as them), and just providing pleasure. To say that art is useful doesn't mean that it isn't also pleasurable. In fact, if we weren't programmed to enjoy art, it couldn't serve its useful functions for us.

Perhaps we can now answer the question of why art as we know it is a trait of humans but not of any other animals. If chimps paint in captivity, why don't they do so in the wild? As an answer, I suggest that wild chimps have their days filled with problems of finding food, surviving, and fending off rival chimp bands. If wild chimps had more leisure time, and the ability to make paints, they would be painting. The proof is that it has already happened: we're still more than 98 percent chimp in our genes.

CHAPTER 8

AGRICULTURE, FOR BETTER AND WORSE

ONE OF OUR DEAREST BELIEFS USED TO BE THAT human history over the last million years was a long tale of progress, of things getting better and better. In particular, agriculture (farming crops and raising domestic animals) was believed to be our clearest step toward a better life. But recent discoveries suggest that agriculture was a milestone for the worse as well as for the better.

Agriculture brought great increases in the amount of food we were able to store. This meant that more people could survive. But agriculture also brought disease, inequality between the sexes and between social classes, and the tyranny of powerful rulers. Among human cultural hallmarks, agriculture is a

(left)
Famine and starvation stalked Ireland in the 1840s, when a plant disease destroyed potato crops. Because people had become dependent on that single food source, as many as a million died.

167

mixed blessing. It is a halfway point between our noble traits, such as language and art, and our vices, such as drug abuse, genocide, and environmental destructiveness.

A Very Recent Development

Compared with other human hallmarks such as language and art, agriculture is especially recent. It began to appear only about ten thousand years ago. Our early steps toward agriculture were not deliberate experiments toward a goal. Humans did not have a plan to domesticate plants and animals. Instead, agriculture grew out of human behaviors and the way plants and animals changed as a result of those behaviors.

Animal domestication arose partly from people keeping captive wild animals as pets and partly from wild animals learning the benefits of staying near people. Wolves, for example, learned to follow human hunters to catch crippled animals that the humans had wounded. People, in turn, sometimes fed or adopted wolf pups. Over time, descendants of some wolves grew tamer and tamer, until they had evolved into domestic dogs. Domestic cats came into existence in a similar way. Once people began harvesting and storing grain, mice and rats learned to raid these food stores. Small wild cats in turn learned that human communities were good places to find mice and rats, and humans learned that cats were useful for getting rid of rodent pests.

Early stages of plant domestication included people harvesting wild plants and throwing out the seeds, which were accidentally "planted." Those seeds would produce more of the edible plants near places where people lived, ate, or looked for food. In time, people began planting seeds on purpose.

The Traditional View of Agriculture

At first, most Americans and Europeans would agree with the traditional view that agriculture was a good thing, a milestone of progress. We enjoy the most abundant and varied foods, the best tools and material goods, and the longest and healthiest lives in human history. Who would really trade that for the life of someone who lived ten thousand years ago?

For most of our history, all humans had to be hunter-gatherers, living by hunting wild animals and gathering wild food plants. According to the traditional view, the hunter-gatherer lifestyle is rugged and short. Because people grow no food and can store only a little, they have no break from the time-consuming struggle to find food and avoid starving, a struggle that starts over again each day. Our escape from this misery came only at the end of the last Ice Age, when people in various parts of the world began independently to domesticate plants and animals. The agricultural revolution gradually spread, until today only a few tribes of hunter-gatherers survive.

In this traditional view of agriculture as progress, no one asks: Why did almost all our hunter-gatherer ancestors adopt agriculture? They adopted it, of course, because it is an efficient way to get more food for less work. Just imagine savage hunters, exhausted from searching for nuts and chasing wild animals, gazing for the first time at a fruit-laden orchard or a pasture full of sheep. How many milliseconds do you think it took those hunters to grasp the advantages of agriculture?

The traditional, progressive view goes further. It gives agriculture credit for the rise of art. Since crops can be stored, and since it takes less time to grow food in gardens than to find it in the jungle, the idea is that agriculture gave us the free time hunter-gatherers never had. We used this free time to create art—agriculture's greatest gift to the human race.

AGRICULTURAL ANTS

NONE OF OUR PRIMATE RELATIVES DOES ANYTHING remotely like agriculture. The closest forerunner of agriculture in the animal world comes from ants, which have domesticated both plants and animals.

Several dozen related species of ants in the Americas are farmers. They cultivate special species of yeasts or fungi in gardens within their nests. Leaf-cutter ants, for example, clip off leaves—but not to eat them. The ants slice the leaves into pieces, scrape off foreign fungi and bacteria, and take the leaf pieces into underground nests. There they crush the leaf fragments into pasty pellets, fertilize them with ant saliva and droppings, and seed them with the ants' preferred species of fungus. This fungus is the ants' main food, sometimes their only food. When a queen ant goes off to found a new colony, she carries with her a starting culture of the precious fungus, just as human pioneers take along seeds to plant.

As for animal domestication, ants obtain a sugary secretion called honeydew from various insects, including grasshoppers, aphids, mealybugs, and caterpillars. These insects are like cows for the ants, which "milk" them by stroking them with their antennae to get the honeydew flowing. In return for the honeydew, the ants protect their "cows" from predators and parasites.

Humans did not, of course, inherit plant and animal domestication directly from ants. Ants evolved it, and later we evolved it separately.

Leaf-cutter ants harvest pieces of leaves that will be used to grow a fungus the ants will eat. The ants are farmers, with leaves as their gardenssoil and fungus as their crop.

The Lives of Hunter-Gatherers

The progressive view tells us that agriculture brought us health, longer lives, security, leisure, and great art. This *seems* convincing, but it is hard to prove. How do you actually show that the lives of people ten thousand years ago got better when they abandoned hunting for farming?

One way is to study the spread of agriculture. If it were such a great idea, you'd expect it to have spread quickly. But archaeology shows that agriculture spread across Europe at a snail's pace— barely a thousand yards per year! From its origins in the Middle East around 8000 BC, agriculture crept northwestward to reach Greece around 6000 BC, and Britain and Scandinavia 2,500 years later. That's hardly what you'd call a wave of enthusiasm.

Another approach is to see whether modern hunter-gatherers are really worse off than farmers. Scattered throughout the world, mainly in areas not good for agriculture, groups such as the Bushmen of southern Africa's Kalahari Desert have continued to live as hunter-gatherers into modern times. Astonishingly, it turns out that these hunter-gatherers generally have leisure time, sleep a lot, and work no harder than their farming neighbors. The average time spent finding food each week, for example, has been reported to be just twelve to nineteen hours

for Bushmen. When asked why he had not adopted agriculture, as neighboring tribes had, one Bushman replied, "Why should we plant, when there are so many mongongo nuts in the world?"

It would be a mistake to swing to the opposite extreme from the traditional, progressive view of agriculture and say that hunter-gatherers lived the life of leisure. Finding food isn't enough. It also has to be made ready to eat, which can take time. But it would also be a mistake to think that hunter-gatherers worked much harder than farmers.

Nutrition is another difference. Farmers concentrate on crops such as rice and potatoes, which are high in carbohydrates. The mixture of wild plants and animals in the hunter-gatherer diet provides more protein and a better balance of other nutrients. Hunter-gatherers are healthy and suffer from little disease. They enjoy a varied diet, and they do not experience the food shortages and famines that can happen to farmers who are dependent on just a few crops. It is almost unimaginable for Bushmen, who use 85 edible wild plants, to starve to death. In the 1840s, however, about a million Irish farmers and their families starved when a plant disease attacked potatoes, which they relied on as their staple crop and food.

(*left*)
A boy of the Moken people. The Moken, or Morgan, are modern hunter-gatherers and skilled divers. These sea nomads travel along coasts in the Indian Ocean and Southeast Asia, living mostly on what they catch and gather, but trading for other goods they need.

Agriculture and Health

Modern hunter-gatherers have lived close to agricultural societies for thousands of years. But what about hunter-gatherers *before* the agricultural revolution. Did the lives of people in the distant past get better after they switched to agriculture?

We can begin to answer that question thanks to paleopathologists, scientists who search for signs of disease in the remains of ancient people. Take the case of historical changes in height. We know that the improved nutrition of modern people has made us taller than people who lived nine or ten centuries ago. We have to stoop, for example, to pass through doorways in medieval castles that were built for a shorter, malnourished population.

A study of skeletons thousands of years old from Greece and Turkey found a striking parallel. The average height of that region's hunter-gatherers in the Ice Age was five foot ten for men, five foot six for women. When people adopted agriculture, height crashed. By 4000 BC, men averaged only five foot three, women five foot one. A few thousand years later, heights were slowly on the rise, but modern Greeks and Turks still do not average the height of their healthy hunter-gatherer ancestors.

Native American hunter-gatherers had skeletons "so healthy it is somewhat discouraging to work with them," as one paleopathologist said. But once Indians began cultivating domestic corn, their skeletons became more interesting. The number of cavities in an average adult's teeth jumped from less than one to nearly seven. Tooth loss became common. Defective enamel in infants' teeth suggests that nursing mothers were severely malnourished. Tuberculosis, anemia, and other diseases increased dramatically. Before corn, 5 percent of the Indian population lived past the age of fifty. After corn, only 1 percent did, and almost one-fifth of the population died between the ages of one and four.

Corn, usually considered one of the blessings of the Americas, was actually a public health disaster. Studies of skeletons elsewhere in the world have led to similar conclusions. The transition from hunting-gathering to farming was bad for public health.

There are at least three explanations for agriculture's negative effects. First, hunter-gatherers enjoyed a varied diet with enough protein, vitamins, and minerals, while farmers ate mostly starchy crops. Even today, just three high-carbohydrate plants—wheat, rice, and corn—provide more than half the calories eaten by the human species. Second, farmers who depended on just one or a few crops ran a greater risk of malnutrition or starvation if one crop failed, as in the case of the Irish potato famine.

Finally, most of today's leading infectious diseases and parasites in humans could not establish themselves until after the switch to agriculture. These killers persist only in societies of crowded, malnourished people who do not move around much and who are constantly reinfected by one another and by their own sewage. Crowd epidemics could not last in small, scattered bands of hunters, who often moved camp. Tuberculosis, leprosy, and cholera had to await the rise of settled farming villages. Smallpox, bubonic plague, and measles appeared only in the last few thousand years, as even denser populations of humans gathered in cities.

THE NEW SCIENCE OF ANCIENT DISEASES

THE LATE TWENTIETH CENTURY SAW THE emergence of a new science: paleopathology. The name comes from the Greek root *paleo*, meaning "ancient," and the science of pathology, which looks for signs of disease. Paleopathologists study the remains of ancient people to see how healthy or unhealthy those populations were.

In some lucky cases, the paleopathologist has a lot to work with. Archaeologists in the deserts of Chile have found mummies so well preserved that scientists could determine their causes of death through autopsies, just as with a fresh corpse in a hospital today. Usually, though, the only remains available for paleopathologists are skeletons. Still, experts can make a surprising number of deductions from skeletal remains.

A skeleton identifies its owner's sex, height and

weight, and approximate age at the time of death. With enough skeletons, researchers can make tables like those used by life insurance companies to calculate a person's expected life span and the risk of death at any age. This tells researchers how long the people in a particular population typically lived.

Paleopathologists can calculate growth rates by measuring bones of people at different ages. Slow growth rates may be a sign that people suffered from hunger or poor nutrition. The scientists also examine teeth for cavities (a sign of a high-carbohydrate diet) or for defects in tooth enamel (a sign of poor nutrition in childhood). Finally, experts interpret the scars left on bones by diseases such as anemia, tuberculosis, leprosy, and osteoarthritis. Through paleopathology, our long-dead ancestors are telling us how they lived—and died.

Class Divisions

Farming brought another curse to humanity: class divisions. Hunter-gatherers have little or no stored food, and no concentrated food sources such as orchards or herds of cows. They live off wild plants and animals that they obtain each day, and everyone except infants, the sick, and the old joins in the search for food. There are no kings, no full-time professional experts, and no social parasites who grow fat off the work of others.

Only a farming population could develop contrasts between the disease-ridden masses and a healthy elite class that is rich or powerful but produces nothing. We see an example of this contrast in skeletons from Greek tombs of around 1500 BC. These remains suggest that royals enjoyed a better diet than commoners. The royal skeletons, for example, were two or three inches taller than those of commoners. Royal mouths contained an average of one cavity or missing tooth, compared with six for the commoners. Something similar shows up in remains from South America. Mummies from three-thousand-year-old cemeteries in Chile show that elites—who were buried with ornaments and gold hair clips—had a rate of bone damage from infectious diseases that was four times lower than the common rate.

To most American and European readers, the idea that humanity could have been better off as hunter-gatherers than we are today sounds ridiculous, because most people in modern industrial societies enjoy better health than hunter-gatherers. They are the elite in today's world, however. They depend on oil and other resources imported from countries that have large peasant populations and much lower health standards.

Some people in industrial and farming societies enjoy more leisure than hunter-gatherers—but this is at the expense of many others who support them and have less leisure. Farming undoubtedly made it possible for societies to support full-time artists and craftspeople, without whom we would not have large-scale art projects such as temples and cathedrals. But great paintings and sculptures on a smaller scale were already being produced by Cro-Magnon hunter-gatherers fifteen thousand years ago, and great art was still produced into modern times by hunter-gatherers such as the Pacific Northwest Indians. And when we think of the specialists whom society became able to support after the shift to agriculture, we should think not just of Shakespeare and Leonardo da Vinci but also of huge armies of professional killers.

A Prehistoric Crossroads

Farming could support far more people than hunting—even if it did not always bring more food to each mouth. Population densities of hunter-gatherers are usually one person or fewer per square mile, while densities of farmers are at least ten times that.

Maybe the main reason we find it hard to shake off the traditional view that agriculture was good for us is that there's no doubt it meant more tons of food per acre. It also meant, however, more mouths to feed. Farming populations grow more quickly than hunter-gatherer ones because women in settled communities typically had a child every two years. Hunter-gatherer women spaced their children four years apart, because a mother must carry her child until it is old enough to keep up with the group.

At the end of the Ice Age ten thousand years ago, some bands took the first steps toward agriculture, which let them feed more mouths.

In time they outbred and then killed off or drove away the bands that chose to remain hunter-gatherers, because ten malnourished farmers can still outfight one healthy hunter. People who did not adopt agriculture were forced out of all areas except the ones that farmers didn't want.

Today, hunter-gatherers linger mainly in places that are useless for agriculture, such as the Arctic and deserts. They are the last people to practice the most successful and long-lasting lifestyle in the history of our species.

Imagine a twenty-four-hour clock, with each hour of clock time representing one hundred thousand years. If the history of the human race began at midnight, we would now be almost at the end of our first day. We lived as hunter-gatherers for almost all that day, from midnight through dawn, noon, and sunset. Finally, at 11:54 p.m., we adopted agriculture. There is no turning back. But as our second midnight approaches, will we find a way to achieve agriculture's blessings while limiting its curses?

CHAPTER 9

WHY DO WE SMOKE, DRINK, AND USE DANGEROUS DRUGS?

OIL SPILLS, CHEMICAL WASTE DUMPS, smog, contaminated food—every month, it seems, we learn of a new way in which we have been exposed to toxic chemicals because of the careless or harmful actions of others. The public feels outrage toward dangerous elements in our environment. Why, then, do so many of us do the same thing to ourselves?

Why do so many people deliberately eat, drink, inject, or smoke dangerous or harmful toxic chemicals such as alcohol, cocaine, and the ingredients in tobacco smoke? Various forms of this willful self-damage are found in many societies today, from primitive tribes to high-tech city-dwellers. Chemical abuse also extends as far back into the past as we have written records. How did drug abuse become a hallmark of the human species?

The Paradox of Self-Destructive Behavior

When something goes against logic or common sense, and yet appears to be true, we call it a paradox. Abuse of toxic chemicals, or any other self-destructive behavior, is a paradox. Why would we do something that we know to be harmful or dangerous?

The mystery isn't in why people continue to take toxic chemicals once they start. They do so because our drugs of abuse are addictive—once you start, the chemistry of the drug affects the brain, making you want to continue. The real mystery is why we start at all.

Most of us are familiar with the overwhelming evidence that alcohol, tobacco, and drugs are destructive, even lethal. Only some strong motive could explain why people consume these poisons voluntarily, even eagerly. It's as if unconscious programs drive us to do something we know to be dangerous. What could those programs be?

There is no single explanation. Different motives drive different people and societies. Some drink to join friends, others to deaden their feelings or drown their sorrows, still others because they like the taste of alcoholic beverages. In addition, the possibilities for achieving a satisfying life are not the same for human populations and social classes, and this explains some patterns in drug use. For example, self-destructive alcoholism is a bigger problem in parts of Ireland that have high rates of unemployment than it is in southeast England.

None of these motives, however, goes to the heart of the paradox: Why do we actively seek what we know to be harmful? I suggest another motive, one that is related to a wide range of seemingly self-destructive traits in animals. It may explain a risky or self-destructive human behavior.

The Clue in the Long Tail

I arrived at this idea while studying an entirely different paradox, one involving bird evolution. While watching a male bird of paradise in New Guinea, I wondered why it had evolved a three-foot-long tail, which surely made it more difficult to fly and walk in the jungle.

Males of other bird of paradise species had evolved other bizarre features, such as long plumes growing out of their eyebrows, brilliant colors, and loud calls. All these features must threaten the birds' survival. Bright colors and loud calls, for example, are likely to attract predatory hawks. Yet those same features serve as advertisements that help the male birds win mates. Like many other biologists, I found myself wondering why male birds of paradise use such handicaps as their advertisements, and why female birds find the handicaps attractive.

At this point I recalled a paper published in 1975 by Amotz Zahavi, an Israeli biologist. Zahavi suggested a new theory about the role of costly or self-destructive signals in animal behavior. His idea was that male traits that make survival more difficult might attract females precisely *because* they are handicaps. Suddenly I realized that Zahavi's idea might apply to the birds of paradise I studied. It could also explain another paradox I had noticed: our use of toxic chemicals, and the way we encourage it in ads that make smoking and drinking look glamorous, even though we know smoking and drinking are destructive.

A Theory about Animal Communication
Zahavi's theory concerned the broad problem of animal communication. Animals need quick,

easily understood signals to convey messages to other animals, including potential mates and predators. Say that a gazelle, for example, notices a lion stalking it. It would be in the gazelle's interest to give a signal that the lion would understand as "I am a superior, fast gazelle! You'll never catch me, so don't waste your time and energy trying." Even if the gazelle really *can* outrun a lion, a signal that discourages the lion saves the gazelle's time and energy, too.

But what signal could the gazelle give? It can't run a demonstration hundred-yard dash in front of every lion that shows up. What about a quick, easy signal, such as pawing the ground with the left hind foot? The problem is that an easy signal opens the door to cheating, because any gazelle, even a slow one, could give the signal. Lions would learn to ignore it. The signal must convince the lion of the gazelle's honesty.

The signal that gazelles use is called stotting. Instead of running away as fast as possible, the gazelle runs slowly, repeatedly jumping high into the air with stiff-legged leaps. At first glance, this behavior appears self-destructive. It wastes time and energy, and it gives the lion a chance to catch up.

Zahavi's theory goes to the heart of this paradox. Signals that put an animal at risk—whether the signals are structures such as long tails or behaviors such as stotting—are good indicators of honesty *because* they are handicaps. A signal that does not cost the signaling animal anything lends itself to cheating, because even a slow or inferior animal can afford to give that signal. Only costly or risky signals guarantee honesty. A slow gazelle that stotted at an approaching lion would seal its fate, but a fast gazelle could outrun the lion even after stotting. By stotting, the gazelle boasts, "I'm so fast that I can escape you even after giving you this head start."

I've described the problem of signals as if the gazelle chooses stotting from many possible behaviors, and as if the lion thinks it over and decides that the stotting is a good sign the gazelle is both speedy and honest. In reality, those "choices" are the result of evolution. They are directed by genes. Gazelles and lions that spare themselves unnecessary, wasteful chases save energy and tend to leave the most offspring. It's a basic principle of evolutionary biology that genetically coded features or behaviors that help

(left)
Why would this young gazelle draw a lion's attention by leaping high into the air? Surprisingly, behavior that looks dangerous or even self-destructive may save an animal's life. All too often, though, instinct drives humans to dangerous behaviors that have no good effects, only destructive ones.

animals leave more offspring—in this case, stotting—get passed on.

Zahavi's theory can be applied to the long tail on that male bird of paradise. Any male bird that has managed to survive in spite of the handicap of a long tail must have terrific genes in other respects. He has proved that he must be *especially* good at finding food, escaping predators, and resisting disease. The bigger the handicap, the harder the test he has passed.

When the female bird of paradise picks a mate, she is like a fairy-tale damsel courted by knights. The damsel tests her suitors by asking them to slay dragons. When she sees a one-armed knight who can *still* slay a dragon, she knows she has found a mate with great genes. By displaying his handicap, the knight or bird of paradise is actually displaying his superiority.

Expensive and Dangerous Human Behavior

It seems to me that Zahavi's theory applies to many costly things humans do to gain status. People who woo possible mates with expensive gifts and other displays of wealth are saying, in effect, "I have plenty of money to support a family. You can believe my boast, because you can see how much money I'm spending now without a care." People who show off jewels or sports cars gain status, because everyone knows that those objects are expensive.

Zahavi's theory can also be applied to more dangerous human behaviors, including the abuse of chemicals. Especially in adolescence and early adulthood, the period when abuse is likely to begin, we devote a lot of energy to establishing our status. I suggest that we share the same unconscious instinct that leads birds and gazelles to indulge in dangerous displays. Ten thousand years ago we "displayed" by challenging a lion or a tribal enemy. Today we do it in other dangerous ways, such as driving fast or consuming dangerous drugs.

THE DANGEROUS DIVES OF MALEKULA'S MEN

AMERICAN INDIANS OF THE PACIFIC NORTHWEST used to seek status by giving away as much wealth as possible in ceremonies known as potlatch rituals. Before modern medicine, tattooing was not only painful but also dangerous because of the risk of infection. Tattooed people were advertising two forms of their strength, tolerance of pain and resistance to disease. These are just two of the many ways people seek status through behavior that is costly, risky, or harmful.

A more dramatic example comes from the Pacific island of Malekula, where men

have traditionally shown off by the insanely
dangerous practice (now imitated around
the world by recreational bungee jumpers)
of building a high tower and then jumping
off it headfirst. The jumper gets a couple
of sturdy vines and ties one end of each
vine to the tower. The other end of each
vine goes around one of the jumper's
ankles. The length of the vines is calculated
to stop the plunge while the jumper's
head is still a few feet above the ground.
Survival demonstrates that the jumper is
courageous, able to do a careful calculation,
and a good builder.

On the Pacific island
of Malekula, part
of the island nation
Vanuatu, young
men tradition-
ally built towers and
then leaped from
them to show their
skill and bravery.
If this jumper has
calculated correctly,
the vines tied to his
ankles will stop him
before he crashes
into the ground.

False Messages

The message of dangerous displays is "I'm strong and superior. I must be strong enough to get past the burning, choking sensation of my first puff on a cigarette, or the misery of my first alcohol-caused hangover. To do it often and remain alive and healthy, I must be superior"— or so I imagine. In reality, although the message of the male bird's long tail is true, for us that message is false. Like so many of our animal instincts, the dangerous display works against us in modern society.

Someone who has smoked several packs of cigarettes a day for years and still hasn't developed lung cancer may have a gene for resistance to lung cancer, but that proves nothing about his or her intelligence, skills, or ability to create a happy life for a spouse and children. In fact, given what we now know about the harmful effects of smoking, that person's behavior may be a sign of negative qualities, such as poor judgment, that would make the smoker a bad choice as a mate.

Animals with brief lives and courtships must develop quick signals. Potential mates don't have enough time to measure each other's real qualities. But humans, with our long lives and courtships and business associations, have plenty of time to study one another's worth. Drug abuse is a classic example of a once-useful instinct that has turned foul in us. In this case, it is the instinct to rely on handicap signals as a sign of strength. Whiskey and cigarette ads are cleverly directed at that old instinct, with their messages that smoking and drinking will bring status and make us attractive. Our buried instinct does not see that these messages are false, but we can use our human abilities to learn, reason, and choose different goals to override the false messages.

Costs and Benefits to Animals and Humans

All animals have had to evolve signals for quickly communicating messages to other animals. To be believable, a signal had to carry some cost, risk, or burden that only superior individuals could afford. Many animal signals that seem to have a negative effect on the signaler— such as stotting in front of a lion, or having a long, burdensome tail in the jungle—can be understood in this light.

This viewpoint may explain the evolution of both human art *and* human chemical abuse. Art and abuse are widespread hallmarks of human society, and it is not immediately obvious how they help us survive or attract mates. I argue in chapter 7 that art often serves as a reliable signal of an individual's superiority or status, because it requires skills to create, and it also requires status or wealth to acquire. Now I'm taking that argument a step further to say that humans seek status through many other costly displays besides art. Some of those displays, such as diving off towers or consuming toxic drugs, are surprisingly dangerous.

I don't claim that this perspective gives us total understanding of either art or chemical abuse. Complex behaviors take on a life of their own and go far beyond their original purpose. At first those behaviors may have served more than one function.

Even from an evolutionary perspective, there remains a basic difference between animal behavior and human chemical abuse. Stotting, long tails, and other animal signals involve costs, but the benefits are greater than the costs. A long-tailed male bird does pay a cost. He has the burden of those feathers when he searches for food or escapes a predator. That cost, however, is more than made up for by the mating advantages the bird gains because his tail attracts females. The end result is more offspring, not fewer, to carry on his genes. The tail only *appears* to be a self-destructive feature. In reality, it favors the survival of the bird's genes.

Human chemical abuse is different. The costs are greater than the benefits. Drug addicts and alcoholics not only lead shorter lives, but they also become *less* attractive, not more, to possible mates. They also lose the ability to care properly for children. Unlike the gazelle's stotting or the bird's long tail, the trait of human chemical abuse does not continue because there are hidden benefits that outweigh the costs. It continues because the toxic substances are chemically addicting. Overall, drinking, smoking, and using drugs are self-destructive behaviors.

Gazelles may occasionally miscalculate in stotting. That's how lions wind up dining on gazelle from time to time. But gazelles don't commit suicide through addiction to the excitement of stotting. Our self-destructive abuse of chemicals has gone beyond its origins in the instinctive behavior of animals.

Average net paid circulation
for September exceeded
Daily --- 1,800,000
Sunday - 3,150,000

Copyright 1938 by News Syndicate Co., Inc. Reg. U. S. Pat. Off.

DAILY  NEWS

NEW YORK'S PICTURE NEWSPAPER

Entered as 2nd class matter, Post Office, New York, N. Y.

FINAL

Vol. 20. No. 109   New York, Monday, October 31, 1938★   48 Pages   2 Cents IN CITY | 3 CENTS LIMITS | Elsewhere

FAKE RADIO 'WAR' STIRS TERROR THROUGH U.S.

—Story on Page 2

"War" Victim

Caroline Cantlon, WPA actress, listening to this radio in West 49th St., heard announcement of "smoke in Times Square." Running to street, she fell, broke her arm.

(NEWS foto)

(By Associated Press)

"I Didn't Know".
Orson Welles, after broadcast expresses amazement at public reaction. He adapted H. G. Wells' "War of the Worlds" for radio and played principal role. Left: a machine conceived for another H. G. Wells story. Dramatic description of landing of weird "machine from Mars" started last night's panic.
—Story on page 2.

CHAPTER 10

ALONE IN A CROWDED UNIVERSE

THE NEXT TIME YOU'RE OUTDOORS ON A CLEAR
night away from city lights, look up at the sky.
Get a sense of the number of stars. Next, find a
pair of binoculars and turn them on the Milky
Way, that stream of brightness across the sky.
See how many more stars are visible now. That
multitude of stars is just the beginning.

Our universe contains billions of galaxies,
each with billions or even trillions of stars.
Many of those stars, we now know, have
planets revolving around them. Once those
numbers have sunk in, you'll be ready to
ask: How could humans possibly be unique
in the universe? How many civilizations of
intelligent beings like us must be out there,
looking back at us? How long before we are in

(left)
In 1938, a radio
broadcast based on
H. G. Wells's novel
War of the Worlds
convinced some
people that the
United States was
being invaded by
Martians. Panic and
confusion reigned
for a few hours.

communication with them, or visit them, or are visited by them?

On Earth, we are unique. No other species possesses language, art, or agriculture remotely close to ours in complexity. Most human hallmarks would not show up at a distance of many light-years. (Distances between stars are measured in light-years. A light-year is the distance light travels in a year, almost six trillion miles). But there *are* two signs of intelligent beings elsewhere that we might be able to detect on Earth, if those beings existed: space probes and radio signals. We are sending out both; other intelligent creatures should be sending them out, too. Where are they?

This seems to me one of the greatest puzzles in science. Given the billions of stars, and given the abilities that developed in our own species, we ought to be detecting the spacecraft, or at least the radio waves, of other species that also developed those abilities. But we have not done so. Could we really be unique, not just on Earth but also in the universe?

COUNTING UP THE ALIEN CIVILIZATIONS

THE FIRST SEARCH FOR EXTRATERRESTRIAL RADIO
signals, in 1960, took place at the National Radio
Astronomy Observatory in Green Bank, West
Virginia. It was carried out by an astronomer named
Frank Drake. The next year Drake arranged a meeting
of scientists at Green Bank to discuss the possibility
of detecting extraterrestrial intelligence. In preparing
for the meeting, Drake created a formula to calculate
how many alien civilizations might exist. Known as
the Green Bank formula, or the Drake equation, it
goes like this:

$$N = R* \cdot fp \cdot ne \cdot fl \cdot fi \cdot fc \cdot L$$

$R*$ = The rate of formation of stars suitable for the
development of intelligent life.

fp = The fraction of those stars with planetary
systems.

ne = The number of planets per solar system with
an environment suitable for life.

"I Didn't Know". Orson Well
broadcast e x
amazement at public reaction. He adapted H. G. W
of the Worlds" for radio and played principal rol
machine conceived for another H. G. Wells story,
description of landing of weird "machine from Ma
last night's panic.
—St

fl = The fraction of suitable planets on which life actually appears.

fi = The fraction of life-bearing planets on which intelligent life emerges.

fc = The fraction of civilizations that develop a technology that releases detectable signs of their existence (such as radio waves) into space.

L = The length of time such civilizations release detectable signals into space.

Astronomers plug their best estimates into each of these variables, using the most recent discoveries or ideas about such things as star formation, the number of stars that have planets, and so on. Multiplied together, the variables produce N, which

is the number of civilizations in our Milky Way galaxy that produce signals we could detect.

The formula suggests a large number of extraterrestrial civilizations. Physicist Enrico Fermi pointed out that based on the formula, we should have been visited by intelligent aliens by now, or at least have detected radio signals from their civilizations—but we have no solid evidence of alien visits or interstellar radio signals. This is called Fermi's paradox.

Some researchers believe that an unknown effect, called the Great Filter, keeps the number of civilizations far lower than expected. Two of the possible Great Filters that have been suggested are that it is very rare for intelligent life to arise, and that technological civilizations don't last very long.

Is There Anybody Out There?

We have already tried to communicate with extraterrestrial life, or life outside Earth. The first attempt came in 1960, when scientists listened (unsuccessfully) for radio transmissions from two nearby stars. Since then, we have sent radio transmissions as well as spacecraft and probes out into space, and we have listened for radio signals that might be a sign of intelligent beings outside our solar system.

Astronomers have tried to calculate the number of advanced civilizations in the universe by using the Green Bank formula, which multiplies a string of estimated numbers, such as the number of stars in the galaxy, the number of those stars that have planets, and the number of those planets that support life. Multiplying all the estimates together, they conclude that the universe must contain billions of billions of planets with life.

A fraction of those life-bearing planets—even if only 1 percent—must have advanced civilizations with the technical skills to send radio signals between the stars. If the Green Bank formula is correct, our galaxy alone must have about a million planets supporting advanced civilizations. So where are they? The silence is deafening.

Something must be wrong with the astronomers' calculations. Astronomers know what they're talking about when they estimate the number of stars and planetary systems, and also the percentage of those systems where life is likely to occur. Instead, the problem may lie in the idea that advanced technical civilizations will evolve on a significant percentage of life-bearing worlds. That idea is based on what biologists call convergent evolution. To understand what convergent evolution means, and its limits, let's look at woodpeckers as a test case.

The Case of the Woodpeckers

Convergent evolution is how biologists describe the fact that many groups of creatures can evolve independently to have the same traits or to occupy the same ecological niche. The evolution of these species converges, or comes to the same place. For example, birds, bats, pterodactyls, and insects all evolved independently to fly. Another example of convergent evolution is eyes, which evolved independently in many different animal groups.

We know that there has been much convergent evolution among species on Earth. There should be some convergence between Earth's species and those elsewhere. Radio communication has evolved here only once, but convergent evolution leads us to expect that it will have emerged on some other planets as well. The group of birds called woodpeckers shows us, however, that convergence is not universal.

Woodpecking is a terrific lifestyle based on digging holes in live wood and prying off pieces of bark to eat tree sap and insects. It means dependable food sources all year

(*left*) An acorn wood-pecker stores food. In spite of the advantages of the woodpecking lifestyle, only one group of creatures on Earth has evolved to follow it. Does this tell us anything about the probability of intelligent life in outer space?

round, and sheltered nest cavities in the holes. Not surprisingly, woodpeckers are very successful birds, widespread over most of the world, with nearly two hundred species, many of them common.

How hard is it to evolve to become a woodpecker? Not very. Woodpeckers are related to several other bird groups. The woodpeckers do have special adaptations for drilling and prying wood. These adaptations include chisel-like bills, nostrils protected with feathers to keep out sawdust, thick skulls, strong neck muscles, and short, stiff tails to press against tree trunks as a brace.

None of the woodpeckers' adaptations is remotely as complicated as building a radio, and all of them are based on features shared by other birds. You might expect the whole package of woodpecking to have evolved repeatedly, with many large groups of animals that drill into live wood for food or nest sites. But nothing else has evolved to enjoy the splendid opportunities of the woodpecker lifestyle. Not all splendid opportunities are seized. If woodpecking evolved only once in the history of life on Earth, should we expect radio building to have evolved more than once in the universe?

Biology and the Evolution of Radios

If radio building were like woodpecking, some species might have evolved certain elements of the package, even if we were the only species to evolve the complete package. We might have found turkeys building transmitters but no receivers, or kangaroos building receivers but no transmitters. The fossil record might reveal five-watt transmitters in the beds of ancient seas, two-hundred-watt transmitters among the bones of the last dinosaurs, and five-hundred-watt transmitters used by sabertoothed cats, until finally humans boosted the power enough to send radio signals into space.

None of that happened. Two centuries ago, modern humans didn't even have the ideas that would lead to radios. The first practical experiments didn't begin until 1888. Only one of the billions of species that have existed on Earth showed any tendency toward radio building, and even that species failed to build a radio for the first 69,999/70,000ths of its

7-million-year history. A visitor from outer space who came to Earth as recently as 1800 would have written off any hope of radios being invented here.

Radios are pretty specific. What about more general qualities necessary to make radios? Chief among those qualities are intelligence and dexterity, which is the ability to control the fine manipulations of objects. Very few animals on Earth have had much of either. No animal has acquired as much of them as humans have.

The only other species that have acquired a little intelligence and dexterity are bonobos and common chimpanzees. In terms of species survival, those two have been rather unsuccessful. Earth's really successful species have been rats and beetles, which are present everywhere in great numbers. But rats and beetles owe their worldwide presence and huge population sizes to things other than intelligence and dexterity.

The Silence Is Deafening—Thank Goodness

The last variable in the Green Bank formula has to do with how long advanced technological civilizations last. The intelligence and dexterity needed to build radios are useful for other purposes, including making devices for destroying the environment and for killing. Here on Earth, we are now stewing in our civilization's juices. Half a dozen countries have the means for bringing us all to a quick end, and other countries are eagerly seeking to get their hands on those means.

It was pure chance that we developed radios at all, and even more of a fluke that we developed radios before we invented the technology that could end us all. Our history suggests that any civilizations that might arise elsewhere are short-lived. They could have reversed their progress overnight, just as we now risk doing.

We're very lucky that that's so. I find it mind-boggling that astronomers who want to spend hundreds of millions of dollars on the search for extraterrestrial life have never thought seriously about what would happen if we found it—or it found us. Would we and the aliens sit down together for fascinating discussions? Would they share their advanced technology with us?

Here, again, our experience on Earth offers useful guidance. We've already found two species that are very intelligent but less technologically advanced than we are: the bonobo and the common chimpanzee. Has our response been to sit down and try to communicate with them? In a few cases, yes, but mostly it has been to shoot them, dissect them, cut off their hands for trophies, put them in cages, infect them with diseases as medical experiments, and destroy or take over their habitats. Throughout history, human explorers who discovered technically less advanced humans responded by shooting them, devastating their populations with new diseases, and destroying or seizing their territory.

Any advanced terrestrials who found us would surely treat us the same way. If there really are any radio civilizations within listening distance of us, let's turn off our own transmitters and try to escape being found, or we're doomed.

Fortunately for us, the silence from outer space is deafening. Out there, in the billions of galaxies with billions of stars, there must be some transmitters, but not many, and they won't last long. What woodpeckers teach us about flying saucers is that we're unlikely ever to see one. For all practical purposes, we're alone in a crowded universe. Thank goodness!

PART FOUR

WORLD
CONQUERORS

LANGUAGE, AGRICULTURE, AND ADVANCED technology are among the cultural hallmarks that make humans unique. They've allowed us to spread over the globe and become world conquerors. In the process of world conquest, our species underwent a basic change in the way different populations of people related to one another. This part of the book explores how and why that change happened—and what it might mean for our future.

Most animal species live across only a small part of the earth's surface. Hamilton's frog, for example, is limited to one forest patch of 37 acres plus one rock pile covering 720 square yards in New Zealand. Humans used to occupy just warm, nonforested areas of Africa. By 50,000 years ago our range— that is, the part of the planet we occupied—was still limited to tropical and warm parts of Africa and Eurasia. Then we expanded to Australia and New Guinea (around 50,000 years ago), cold parts of Europe (by 30,000 years ago), Siberia (by 20,000 years ago), North and South America (around 11,000 years ago), and Polynesia (between 3,600 and 1,000 years ago). Today we occupy or at least visit all lands and the surface of all the oceans, and we are starting to probe into space and the ocean's depths.

Our expansion didn't just mean moving

(left and previous spread) Members of the Archbold Expedition atop their seaplane on a New Guinea lake. This 1938 expedition broke the long isolation of the Dani people, who had lived in the Grand Valley of western New Guinea, unknown to the outside world, for centuries.

into unoccupied areas. It also involved human populations conquering, driving out, or killing other human populations. Some groups colonized the territory of others, settling on the land and taking military or political control of it. We became conquerors of one another as well as of the world. Our expansion reveals another human hallmark: our tendency to kill members of our own species in large numbers. This grew out of traits found in the animal world, but we've taken it far beyond its animal limits. Our tendency to kill one another is one of the possible reasons that our species might fall.

In the next three chapters we'll see how the expansion of our range led to a flowering of languages and cultures. We'll explore the question of why some people gained advantages that let them conquer other people, and we'll examine one of the largest shifts in recent history: the expansion of modern Europeans into the Americas and Australia.

Finally, we'll look at one of humanity's darker traits, xenophobia, which is fear of people who are different from us. Xenophobia has roots in the competition that occurs everywhere in the animal world, but only humans have developed weapons that can kill large numbers of our own species at a distance. A look at the history of human genocide shows the ugly tradition that gave rise to the horrors of modern war.

CHAPTER II

THE LAST FIRST CONTACTS

A LONG STAGE OF HUMAN HISTORY DREW CLOSER
to its end on August 4, 1938. On that date a
scientific expedition from the American Museum
of Natural History became the first outsiders to
enter the western part of the Grand Valley in New
Guinea, a long, lush valley hidden from the island's
coasts by steep walls of knife-edged, jungle-covered
mountain ridges. The area was long thought to
be uninhabited, but to everyone's astonishment,
the valley proved to be densely populated by fifty
thousand people living in the Stone Age. No one
had known they existed, and they had no idea that
there were other people and an outside world.

The scientific expedition had traveled
into the interior of New Guinea to search for

unknown birds and mammals. It found an unknown human society, now known as the Dani people. The 1938 entry into the Grand Valley was one of the last first contacts between an advanced culture and a large population with no knowledge of the outside world. It was a landmark in the process by which humanity changed from thousands of tiny societies to world conquerors with world knowledge. To see the significance of that 1938 meeting, we need to understand what "first contact" means—and how it has changed human societies.

The World before First Contact

Most animal species occupy a geographic range that is limited to a small fraction of the earth's surface. When animals do occur on several continents, individuals from the different continents do not visit each other. Instead, each continent, and usually each small part of a continent, has its own distinctive population. That population has contacts with its close neighbors but not with distant members of the same species.

The fact that populations have limited geographic ranges is reflected in geographic variations within species. Populations of the same species in different geographic areas tend to evolve into different-looking subspecies, because most breeding remains within the same population. For example, there are two subspecies of lowland gorillas in Africa: eastern and western. No East African lowland gorilla has ever turned up in West Africa, and no West African lowland gorilla has been seen in East Africa. Although they belong to the same species, the two subspecies look different enough for biologists to be able to identify them on sight.

Humans have been typical animals throughout most of our evolutionary history, meaning that populations of people have tended to remain inside distinct geographical areas. Each human population became genetically molded to its area's climate and diseases. In addition, differences in language and culture kept humans from freely mixing.

We think of ourselves as travelers, but we were just the opposite for several million years. Every human group was ignorant of the world beyond its own lands and those of its immediate neighbors. While most peoples had trade relations with their neighbors, some groups thought they were the only humans in existence.

Perhaps the smoke of fires on the horizon, or an empty canoe floating down the river, proved the existence of other people. But to venture out of one's own territory to meet those strangers, even if they lived only a few miles away, seemed suicidal. Groups had a no-trespassing mentality. The notion of accepting unrelated strangers was as unthinkable as the idea that such a stranger might show up on your doorstep.

Only in the past few thousand years have changes in political systems and technology allowed some people to travel far, to meet people of other cultures, and to learn about places and peoples they had not personally visited. This process speeded up with Christopher Columbus's arrival in the Americas in 1492. Today there remain only a few tribes, in New Guinea and South America, that still await their first contact with remote outsiders. Yet the world before first contact—a world that is finally ending within our generation—holds the key to the great diversity in human cultures.

Isolation and Diversity

Today, thanks to the Internet, movies, and TV, we can picture parts of the world we haven't visited.

We can read about them in books. Language barriers no longer block the flow of information. Most villages that still speak minor languages contain at least one person who speaks one of the world's major languages, such as English. Almost every village in the world has received fairly direct accounts of the outside world, and has given the outside world accounts of itself.

Precontact peoples had no way to picture the outside world or learn about it directly. Information arrived, if it arrived at all, by way of long chains of accounts passed along by many people, translated into various languages along the way, with accuracy lost at each step. The highlanders of New Guinea, for example, knew nothing of the ocean a hundred miles away, or of the white men who had been prowling their coasts for several centuries. First contact had a powerful effect on the highlanders—one that is hard for those of us living in the modern world to imagine.

First contact revolutionized the highlanders' material culture by bringing such items as steel axes, which were immediately recognized as better than stone axes. Later came missionaries and government administrators, who changed the highlanders' culture by ending long-standing practices such as cannibalism, tribal war, and marriage of one man to multiple wives. Tribespeople sometimes voluntarily gave up their old ways in favor of the new goods and practices they saw. But there was also a deeper revolution in the highlanders' view of the universe. They and their neighbors were no longer the only humans, with the only way of life.

The scientists' entry into the Grand Valley in 1938 was a turning point for the Dani. It was also part of a turning point in human history. What difference did it make that all human groups used to live in relative isolation, waiting for first contact, while only a few such groups remain today? To glimpse the answer to that question, we can compare places whose isolation ended long ago with areas where groups remained isolated into modern times. We can also study the rapid changes that have followed first contacts throughout history. These comparisons suggest that contact between distant peoples gradually wiped out much of the cultural diversity that had developed during thousands of years of isolation.

(right)
A Dani man and children page through a Western guidebook to New Guinea.

ART IN FLAMES

FOR A GOOD EXAMPLE OF HOW ISOLATION increases cultural diversity, while contact means less cultural diversity, we can look at the range of art in New Guinea before and after contact with the rest of the world.

Styles of sculpture, music, and dance used to vary greatly from village to village. Some villagers along the Sepik River and in the Asmat swamps produced wood carvings that are now world-famous because of their quality. But New Guinea villagers have been increasingly pressured or lured into abandoning their artistic traditions. When I visited an isolated small tribe of 578

people in 1965, for example, the missionary who controlled the only store had just manipulated the people into burning all their art—which he called "heathen artifacts."

On my first visit to remote New Guinea villages in 1964, I heard log drums and traditional songs. On my visits in the 1980s, I heard guitars, rock music, and battery-operated boom boxes. Anyone who has seen the Asmat carvings at New York's Metropolitan Museum of Art, or who has heard a duet played on log drums at breathtaking speed, can appreciate the enormous tragedy of art lost after first contact.

Artworks such as this carving (made in New Guinea in the late nineteenth or early twentieth century) are prized by collectors and museums—but many have been destroyed, and the art of making them lost, as the diversity of cultures around the world shrinks.

The Extinction of Languages

Cultural diversity is represented in diversity of languages—and there has been a massive loss of languages. Europe today has about fifty languages. Most of them belong to a single family of languages, called Indo-European. In contrast, New Guinea, with less than one-tenth of Europe's area and less than one-hundredth of its population, has hundreds of languages. Many of them are unrelated to any other known language in New Guinea or elsewhere! The average New Guinea language is spoken by a few thousand people who live within ten miles of each other.

That's what the world used to be like, with each isolated tribe having its own language, until the rise of agriculture allowed a few groups to expand and spread their language over large areas. It was only about six thousand years ago that the Indo-European language family began to expand, leading to the end of almost all earlier languages in western Europe. The same thing happened in Africa within the last few thousand years, when the Bantu language family exterminated most other languages of Africa south of the Sahara Desert. In North and South

America, hundreds of Indian languages have become extinct in recent centuries.

Isn't language loss a good thing, because fewer languages make it easier for the world's people to communicate? Maybe, but it's a bad thing in other ways. Languages differ in structure and vocabulary. They also differ in how they express feelings, relationships among events, and personal responsibility. They differ in how they shape our thoughts. There's no single "best" language. Instead, different languages are better suited for different purposes. When a language goes extinct, we lose a window into the unique worldview of the people who once spoke it.

Alternative Models of Human Society

The range and diversity of cultural practices in New Guinea is greater than that of same-size areas elsewhere in the modern world, because isolated tribes were able to live out social experiments that others would find unacceptable. Forms of self-mutilation and cannibalism, for example, varied from tribe to tribe. Child-rearing practices ranged from extreme permissiveness, through punishment of misbehavior by rubbing a child's face with stinging nettles, to repression so strict that it led to child suicides.

Among one group, the Barua, men lived with young boys in a single large house, while each man had a separate house for his wife, daughters, and infant sons. The Tudawhes, in contrast, had two-story houses in which women, babies, unmarried girls, and pigs lived on the lower level, while men and unmarried boys lived on the upper level that they entered by a separate exterior ladder.

If the loss of cultural diversity in the modern world meant only the end of self-mutilation and child suicide, we wouldn't mourn it. But the societies whose cultural practices now dominate the globe owe that domination to their economic and military success. These qualities aren't necessarily the ones that encourage happiness or promote long-term human survival.

Our consumerism and environmental exploitation may serve us well now, but they are not good signs for our future. Features of American society that already rate as disasters in anyone's book include our treatment of old people, adolescent turmoil and stress, abuse of toxic chemicals, and inequality. For each of these problems, there are—or were, before first contact—many New Guinea societies that found far better solutions.

These alternative models of human society, unfortunately, are rapidly disappearing. Surely there are no remaining uncontacted populations as large as that of New Guinea's Grand Valley. When I worked on New Guinea's Rouffaer River in 1979, missionaries had just found a tribe of four hundred nomads who reported another uncontacted band five days' travel up the river. In 2011, filmmakers in airplanes captured on video small bands of uncontacted tribespeople in the Amazon rain forest, on the border between Peru and Brazil. Small bands such as those continue to turn up. But at some point within the early twenty-first century, we can expect the last first contact, and the end of the last separate experiment at designing human society.

That last first contact won't mean the end of cultural diversity. Much cultural diversity, in fact, has proven able to survive television, travel, and the Internet. But the shift from isolated groups to a global population does mean a drastic loss of diversity. That loss is to be mourned, but there is also a positive side. The fact that our cultures are blending and growing more like one another is cause for hope. Our xenophobia—our fear and hatred of strangers—was manageable only as long as we lacked the means to destroy ourselves as a species. Now that we possess nuclear weapons, it may be best that we learn to see ourselves as members of a shared worldwide culture. Loss of cultural diversity may be the price we have to pay for survival.

CHAPTER 12

ACCIDENTAL CONQUERORS

A LITTLE MORE THAN FIVE HUNDRED YEARS ago, everyone in the Americas was an American Indian. Everyone in Australia was a native Australian, or aboriginal. How did people from Europe come to replace almost all the native people of the Americas and Australia?

To put it another way, why did technology and political organization develop fastest in Eurasia, slower in the Americas and in Africa south of the Sahara Desert, and slowest in Australia? In 1492 much of the population of Eurasia used iron tools, had writing and agriculture, lived in large centralized states with oceangoing ships, and was on the verge of developing industry. The Americas had agriculture, only a few large centralized states, writing in only one area, and no oceangoing ships or iron tools. Australia had no agriculture, writing, states, or ships. Its people used stone tools like the ones used ten thousand years earlier in Eurasia.

Nineteenth-century Europeans had a simple, racist answer to those questions. They credited their cultural head start to their being more intelligent than other peoples. They also believed it was their destiny to conquer, displace, or kill "inferior" peoples. This answer is not just loathsome and arrogant; it is also wrong. People differ enormously in the knowledge they gain depending on the circumstances in which they grow up. But no good evidence of genetic differences in mental ability among peoples of different races or cultures has ever been found. Europeans expanded into other continents, and not the other way around, because of technological and political differences, not biological or racial superiority.

Geography and Civilization

If there are no genetic differences in mental ability among peoples who originated on different continents, why did civilization develop at such different rates around the world? The answer, I think, is geography. Continents differed in the resources on which civilization depended— especially the wild plant and animal species that became crops and domestic animals. In some continents these useful species could spread from one region to another more easily than in other continents. Geography and biogeography, which is the pattern of species and ecosystems as they are distributed across various regions, have been molding human lives for thousands of years.

Why do I emphasize plant and animal species? Agriculture and herding brought the disadvantages I describe in chapter 8, but they also made it possible to feed far more people for each square mile of land. Extra food grown by some people and stored to feed others meant that those other individuals could devote themselves to metalworking, manufacturing, writing, and soldiering. Domestic animals provided not only meat and milk to feed people but also wool and hides to clothe them, and power to move people and goods. And by pulling plows and carts, animals made agriculture much more productive than when the only power source was human muscle.

As a result of agriculture and herding, the human population rose from about ten million in 10,000 BC, when we were all hunter-gatherers, to more than seven billion today. Dense populations were needed for centralized states to rise. Dense populations also led to the evolution of infectious diseases. Some populations exposed to these diseases developed resistance to them, while others did not. All these factors determined who conquered and colonized whom.

Europeans did not conquer the Americas and Australia because they had better genes. They conquered because they had worse germs (especially smallpox), more advanced technology (including weapons and ships), information storage through writing, and political organization. All these things stemmed from continental differences in geography.

Different Domestic Animals

By around 4000 BC, people in western Eurasia already had the "Big Five" domestic livestock animals that are still the most common: sheep, goats, pigs, cows, and horses. East Asians domesticated four other cattle species that replace cows in various regions: yaks, water buffalo, gaur, and banteng. Together, these domestic animals provided food, power, and clothing. In addition, the horse was of enormous military value. It was the tank, truck, and jeep of warfare until the nineteenth century.

Why didn't American Indians domesticate similar native American species: mountain sheep, mountain goats, peccaries (wild relatives of pigs), bison, and tapirs? Why didn't Indians mounted on tapirs, and native Australians astride battle kangaroos, invade and terrorize Eurasia?

The answer is that it has proved possible to domesticate only a few of the world's animal species. Many species have reached the first step: being kept captive as tame pets. In New Guinea villages, I routinely find tame possums and kangaroos. I saw tame monkeys and weasels in Amazonian villages. Ancient Egyptians tamed gazelles, antelopes, cranes, and even hyenas and possibly giraffes. Ancient Romans were terrorized by the tamed African elephants with which the general Hannibal crossed the Alps.

But all these attempts at domestication finally failed. Domestication means more than capturing individual wild animals and training them to behave tamely. Domestication means breeding animals in captivity—and not just breeding them, but choosing which individuals to breed so that their offspring will have desirable features, such as a gentle temper, thick wool, or a willingness to carry loads. By breeding domestic animals over time, choosing individual animals with certain traits, humans turn a wild species into one that is more useful to them.

Horses were domesticated around 4000 BC, reindeer a few thousand years later. Since then, no large European mammal has been domesticated. Our few modern species of domestic mammals are those that remain after many others were tried and abandoned.

For domestication to succeed, a wild animal must have certain characteristics. First, in most cases, the animal must be a social animal— which means one that lives in herds or packs. These animals instinctively submit to the dominant animals in their herds or packs, and they can transfer this submissive behavior from animal leaders to humans. In other words, the human owner of a social animal becomes the top animal in the pecking order. Social animals are hardwired to interact with others, even if those others happen belong to a different species. Cats and ferrets are the only solitary, nonsocial animals that have been domesticated.

Second, animals such as deer that instantly

take flight at the first sign of danger, rather than standing their ground, are too nervous to domesticate. Of the world's dozens of deer species, reindeer are the only ones that have been successfully domesticated. The others were eliminated as possibilities because of their flight reflexes, their territorial instincts, or both.

Finally, as zoos often discover to their dismay, captive animals may refuse to breed in cages or pens, even if they are well fed and healthy. The problem of getting captive animals to breed has ruined attempts to domesticate some potentially useful species. The finest wool in the world comes from the vicuna, a relative of the camel that lives in the Andes Mountains of South America. No rancher has ever been able to domesticate it, so wool is still obtained by capturing wild vicunas. Princes from the ancient Middle East to nineteenth-century India captured and tamed cheetahs, wild cats that are the world's fastest land mammals, to use in hunting. But every hunting cheetah had to be captured from the wild, then tamed. Even zoos were unable to breed cheetahs in captivity until the 1960s.

Together, these reasons help explain why Eurasians succeeded in domesticating the Big

Five but not other closely related species, and why American Indians did not domesticate peccaries or bison.

The Revolutionary Horse

Horses, with their high military value, show how small differences can make one species prized while another species is useless. Horses belong to the order of animals called Perissodactyla, which includes hoofed mammals with an odd number of toes. Horses, tapirs, and rhinoceroses all belong to this order. Of the seventeen living species of Perissodactyla, all four tapirs and all five rhinos, plus five of the eight wild horse species, have never been domesticated. Africans or American Indians mounted on fighting rhinos would have trampled European invaders—but it never happened.

A sixth wild horse relative, the wild ass of Africa, gave rise to domestic donkeys, which proved splendid as pack animals but useless as military chargers. The seventh wild horse relative, the onager of western Asia, may have been used to pull wagons for a few centuries in ancient times, but all descriptions mention its vicious temper. As soon as Asians could replace them with domesticated horses, they gave up trying to use the troublesome onagers.

Horses revolutionized warfare in a way that no other animal, not even elephants or camels, ever rivaled. Hitched to battle chariots, horses became the unstoppable tanks of the ancient world. After the invention of saddles and stirrups made it easier for people to ride horses, cavalry (soldiers mounted on horseback) became a vital military asset. The mounted warriors of Attila the Hun devastated the Roman Empire, the riders of Mongol leader Genghis Khan conquered an empire that stretched across Russia and China, and military kingdoms with cavalry troops arose in West Africa.

A few dozen horses helped the Spanish conquistadors Cortés and Pizarro, each leading only a few hundred Spanish fighters, overthrow the two most populated and advanced American states: the Aztec Empire in Mexico and the Inca Empire in South America. The military importance of this most universally prized of all domestic animals finally ended after six thousand years, in September 1939, when Polish cavalry riders spurred their steeds into doomed charges against the invading German armies of Adolf Hitler.

EXTINCTIONS THAT SHAPED HISTORY

IN THE SIXTEENTH CENTURY, HORSES HELPED the Spanish conquistadors Cortés and Pizarro conquer the two most powerful empires in the Americas: the Aztecs and the Incas. Because the Americas had no native horses, Aztec and Inca warriors were unprepared for the terrifying sight of conquistadors mounted on charging steeds. Wild horses similar to the ancestors of the conquistadors' horses, however, had once been native to the Americas. If those American horses had survived, the Aztec and Inca leaders might have surprised the Spanish invaders with cavalry charges of their own. But, in a cruel twist of fate, America's horses had become extinct long before, along with 80 to 90 percent of the other large mammal species of the Americas. (Wild horses in the Americas today descended from herds brought by European explorers and settlers.)

The mass mammal extinction happened around the same time that the first human settlers, the ancestors of modern Indians, reached the American continents. The Americas lost not only horses but other species that might have been domesticated, including large camels, ground sloths, and elephants. The same thing happened in Australia, where large mammals disappeared around the time the first people arrived. Australia and North America wound up with no domestic species at all, unless the Indians' dogs were the descendants of North American wolves. South America was left with only the guinea pig (used for food), a relative of the camel called the alpaca (used for wool), and another camel relative called the llama (used for carrying loads, but too small to carry a rider).

No native American or Australian mammal ever pulled a plow, a cart, or a war chariot.

ntra el Exercito de CORTÉS triunfante en Tlas
despues de la Victoria de Otumba.

None ever gave milk or carried a rider. After the civilizations of Eurasia and Africa had harnessed the power of animal muscle, wind, and water, the civilizations of the Americas limped forward on human muscle power alone.

As you'll see in part 5 of this book, scientists still debate whether hunting by the first human settlers in Australia and the Americas caused the mass extinction of large mammals in those continents. Whatever the cause, the extinctions made it almost certain that the descendants of those first Australians and Americans would be conquered, thousands of years later, by people from Eurasia and Africa—the continents that kept most of their large mammal species.

(right, above, and previous spread) Spanish conquistador Hernán Cortés rides triumphantly into a Mexican city. Mounted warfare helped the Spanish overthrow the powerful Aztec and Inca states in the Americas, where horses were unknown.

Plant Power

Plant foods played a vital role in the rise of civilizations. In fact, most of the calories consumed by the human race still come from plants—specifically, from cereals, which are grasses with edible starchy seeds, such as barley kernels or wheat grains. But as with animals, only a tiny fraction of all wild plant species has proved suitable for domestication.

Why were some plants easier to domesticate than others? For one thing, some plants are self-pollinators, which means that a single individual plant can pollinate itself, or fertilize its own seeds. These plants, including wheat, can produce their offspring on their own. Other plants, such as rye, are cross-pollinators, meaning that pollen from one plant must reach a different plant. Self-pollinators were domesticated earlier and more easily than cross-pollinators. People found it easier to select and maintain desirable strains of self-pollinators, because these plants did not constantly mix with their wild relatives, as cross-pollinators did.

Australia was relatively poor in native plants suitable for domestication. That may explain

(left)
Next to a quarter, an ear of teosinte (left) is much smaller than an ear of modern corn (right). It took thousands of years for the major grain of the Americas to evolve into a form that could support large populations.

why the aboriginal Australians never developed agriculture. But it's not so obvious why agriculture in the New World of the Americas lagged behind agriculture in the Old World of Eurasia and Africa. After all, many food plants that are now important around the world originated in the New World: corn, potatoes, tomatoes, and squash, to name just a few. The answer to the puzzle calls for a closer look at corn, the New World's most important crop.

All civilizations have depended on cereals, but different civilizations have domesticated different cereals. In the Middle East and Europe, the grains were wheat, barley, oats, and rye. In China and Southeast Asia, they were rice, foxtail millet, and broomcorn millet. In Africa south of the Sahara Desert, they were sorghum, pearl millet, and finger millet. But in the New World, only corn.

Soon after Columbus's voyage to America, early explorers took corn back to Europe. It spread around the globe, so that now more acres are planted in corn than in any other cereal except wheat. Corn is the most important crop in the United States today. Why, then, didn't corn let the civilizations of the American Indians develop as fast as the Old World civilizations that were fed by wheat and other cereals?

Corn was a much bigger pain in the neck to domesticate and grow, and it gave an inferior product. Those will be fighting words if you, like me, love hot buttered corn on the cob. Hear me out on the differences between corn and other cereals.

The Old World had more than a dozen wild grasses that were easy to domesticate and to grow. These grasses had large seeds. It was easy to harvest many stalks at a time with sickles, easy to grind the seeds and prepare them for cooking, and easy to sow seeds for next year's crop. These grains were already productive in the wild. You can still harvest up to seven hundred pounds of grain from each acre of wild wheat growing naturally on Middle Eastern hillsides. In a few weeks a family could harvest enough to feed itself for a year. Even before wheat and barley were domesticated, villages had invented sickles, mortars and pestles for grinding, and pits for storing grain. They supported themselves on wild grains.

Domesticating wheat and barley wasn't a conscious act. A group of hunter-gatherers didn't sit down one day, mourn the extinction of big-game animals, and decide to become wheat farmers. Instead, plant domestication was an unplanned result of people's preferring some wild plants over others and accidentally spreading seeds of the plants they preferred. In the case of cereals, people preferred plants with big seeds that were easy to remove from the seed coverings, and with firm stalks that held the seeds and kept them from scattering.

It took only a few mutations, which people then favored, to turn wild grasses into domestic cereals. Archaeological digs at Middle Eastern sites show that these changes began to appear in wheat and barley around 8000 BC. Two thousand years later, crop cultivation had been combined with animal herding to create a complete food production system in the Middle East. For better or worse, people were no longer hunter-gatherers. They were farmers and herders, on the way to becoming civilized.

Contrast this with what happened in the New World. The parts of the Americas where farming began did not have large-seeded wild grasses that were already productive in the wild. The ancestor of corn was a wild grass that did have big seeds, but in other ways hardly seemed like a promising food plant. It is called teosinte. No other crop underwent such drastic changes on the way to being domesticated. Teosinte has only six to twelve kernels per ear, and they are enclosed in stone-hard cases. No one uses these seeds today, and there is no sign that anyone did in prehistoric times, either.

The key to making teosinte useful was a sex change! In teosinte the side branches end in tassels made of male flowers. In corn, these branches end in female structures, the ears. This sounds like a drastic difference, but it's really a simple hormonal change that could have been started by a fungus, virus, or a change in climate. Once some flowers on the tassel had changed to female, they would have produced edible, exposed grains likely to catch the eye of hungry hunter-gatherers. The central branch of the tassel would then have been the beginning of a corncob. Early Mexican archaeological sites have yielded remains of cobs barely an inch and a half long.

Thousands of years of development still lay ahead before corn yielded enough grain to support cities or even villages. The final product was still much more work for farmers than the

Old World grains. Corn ears had to be harvested individually by hand, rather than in bunches with a sickle. The kernels didn't simply fall off like grain but had to be scraped or bitten off the cob. Sowing the seeds involved planting them individually rather than scattering handfuls. And the result was poorer nutritionally than Old World grains—corn had less protein and was deficient in niacin and important amino acids.

Compared with Old World cereals, the main food crop of the New World was much harder to recognize as useful in the wild, harder to domesticate, and harder to use even after it was domesticated. Much of the lag between New World and Old World civilizations may be due to the peculiar features of a single plant.

North–South versus East–West

Biogeography—the way different plant and animal species are distributed over the world—determined which wild species were available for people to domesticate in a given area. Geography also played another major role in human history.

Each civilization has depended not only on the food plants it domesticated, but also on other food plants that arrived after first having been domesticated somewhere else. The spread of food plants was affected by the different shapes of the Old and New Worlds. The mainly north–south axis, or central line, of the New World made it hard for food plants to spread over large areas. The mainly east–west axis of the Old World made it easy. Here's why:

Plants and animals spread quickly and easily within a climate zone they're already adapted to. In order to spread out of that zone and into other climates, they have to develop new varieties that tolerate different conditions. A glance at the map shows that Old World plants and animals could shift long distances without encountering a change in climate. Species moved between China, India, the Middle East, and Europe without ever leaving the temperate part of the Northern Hemisphere.

Related grains came to stretch for seven thousand miles, from the English Channel to the China Sea. The ancient Romans grew wheat and barley from the Middle East, peaches and citrus fruits from China, cucumbers and sesame from India, and hemp and onions from central Asia, along with local oats and poppies. Horses that spread from the Middle East to West Africa revolutionized military tactics there. African sorghum and cotton reached India by 2000 BC, while bananas and yams from tropical Southeast Asia crossed the Indian Ocean to enrich agriculture in tropical Africa.

But in the New World, the temperate zone of North America is isolated from the temperate zone of South America by thousands of miles of tropics, where temperate-zone species can't survive. The domesticated llama, alpaca, and guinea pig of the South American Andes never spread to Mexico or North America. Potatoes also failed to spread from the Andes to North America, while sunflowers never spread from North America to the Andes. Even crops that were grown in both North and South America in prehistoric times—including cotton, beans, chili peppers, and tomatoes—existed in different varieties or even species on the two continents, which suggests that they were domesticated independently in both areas.

Corn did spread from Mexico to North and South America, but it evidently wasn't easy, perhaps because it took time to develop varieties for different climates. Not until 900 AD, thousands of years after corn emerged in Mexico, did it become a staple food in the Mississippi Valley. The arrival of corn triggered the rise of the mysterious mound-building civilization of the American Midwest.

Imagine reversing the shapes of the two hemispheres. If the Old World had had a north–south axis, and the New World had had an east–west axis, the spread of domestic crops and animals would have been slower in the Old World and faster in the New World. Who knows whether that difference would have been enough to let the Aztecs or the Incas invade Europe?

Geography Sets the Ground Rules

The fact that civilizations rose faster on some continents than on others was not an accident caused by a few geniuses. And it wasn't due to differences in intelligence or in inventiveness from one human population to the next—there is no evidence of such differences, anyway. Biogeography led to the differences in cultural development. If Europe and Australia had exchanged their entire human populations twelve thousand years ago, it would have been the former Australians, transplanted to Europe, who would eventually have invaded the Americas and Australia.

Geography sets ground rules for the biological and cultural evolution of all species, including our own. Geography has also played a role in shaping our modern political history. Disasters have been caused by politicians ignorant of geography. In the nineteenth century, the European powers that colonized Africa divided up the continent into territories. Later, when the territories became independent nations, they inherited those borders—which often had no relation to the geography, ethnic relationships, or economies of the African people.

In the same way, when the Treaty of Versailles ended World War I in 1919, politicians drew new borders for eastern Europe. Unfortunately, the politicians knew little of the region. The national borders they forced on it helped fuel World War II a generation later. A few weeks spent studying geography in seventh grade is not enough to teach our future politicians the effects that maps have on us. In the long run, and on a broad scale, where we live contributes heavily to making us who we are.

CHAPTER 13

IN BLACK AND WHITE

IN 1988 AUSTRALIA CELEBRATED ITS
two-hundredth anniversary. The modern
nation of Australia had begun as a colony fifteen
thousand miles from the home country of
England. Many of the colonists were convicts
sent on the eight-month voyage to Australia as
punishment. They had no idea what to expect
or how to survive in their new home. Two
and a half years of near starvation would pass
before a supply fleet arrived. Despite these grim
beginnings, the settlers survived, prospered, and
built a democracy. It's no wonder Australians felt
pride as they celebrated their nation's founding.

Yet protests marred the celebrations. The
white settlers were not the first Australians.

Fifty thousand years earlier, the continent had been settled by the ancestors of the dark-skinned people usually called Aborigines, also known in Australia as blacks. In the course of English settlement, most of these original inhabitants were killed or died of disease. For this reason some of their modern descendants staged protests, not celebrations, to mark the two-hundredth year since the white settlers arrived. Why did Australia stop being black, and how did the courageous English settlers come to commit the crime we call genocide, a deliberate attempt to exterminate a whole people?

Genocide: A Human Invention?

The white settlers in Australia were not the only ones to commit the horrendous offense of genocide. Instead, it has happened more frequently than most people realize. When they hear the term *genocide*, many think of Nazi Germany in the mid-twentieth century, when mass killings of Jews and other minorities took place in concentration camps during World War II. But those killings were not even the largest genocide of that century.

Hundreds of groups have been targets of successful extermination campaigns. Numerous groups scattered throughout the world are potential targets for the near future. Yet genocide is such a painful subject that we'd rather not think about it at all, or else we'd like to believe that nice people don't commit genocide—only Nazis do. But our refusal to think about genocide has serious consequences. We've done little to halt the many genocides since World War II, and we're not alert to where one might happen next.

Basic questions about genocide remain in dispute. Do any animals routinely kill large numbers of their own species, or is that a human invention? Has genocide been rare throughout human history, or has it been common enough to rank as a human hallmark, along with art and language? Is genocide becoming more common, because modern weapons allow push-button slaughter at a distance, reducing our instinctive reluctance to kill? Finally, are genocidal killers abnormal individuals, or are they normal people placed in unusual situations?

Before we search for answers to these questions, it is useful to look at a case study: the extermination of the Tasmanians.

Extermination Down Under

Tasmania is a mountainous island about the size of Ireland. It lies a hundred and fifty miles off Australia's southeast coast. When Europeans discovered Tasmania in 1642, the island was home to about five thousand hunter-gatherers.

These Tasmanians were related to the Aborigines of Australia. Their technology might have been the simplest of that of any modern people. They made only a few simple stone and wooden tools. Unlike the Aborigines, Tasmanians did not have boomerangs, dogs, nets, sewing, or the ability to start a fire. Unable to make long sea journeys, they had had no contact with other people since rising sea levels separated Tasmania and Australia ten thousand years ago. When the white colonists of Australia finally ended that isolation, no two peoples on earth were less equipped to understand each other than Tasmanians and whites.

The tragic collision of these two peoples led to conflict almost as soon as British seal hunters and settlers arrived around 1800. Whites kidnapped Tasmanian women and children, killed men, trespassed on hunting grounds, and tried to clear Tasmanians off their land. By 1830 the native population of northeast Tasmania was reduced to seventy-two men, three women, and no children. In one example of violence, four white shepherds ambushed a group of natives, killed thirty people, and threw their bodies over a cliff that some Australians today call Victory Hill.

Naturally, Tasmanians fought back, and whites fought even harder in turn. The white governor tried to end the violence by ordering all Tasmanians to leave the parts of their island where whites had settled. Soldiers were authorized to kill any natives in the settled areas. A missionary rounded up the surviving Tasmanians and moved them to a small nearby island. Many Tasmanians died, but about two hundred of them, the last survivors of the former population of five thousand, reached Flinders Island. The settlement there was run like a jail, and its occupants suffered from malnutrition and illness. By 1869 only three remained alive. The last full Tasmanian, a woman named Truganini, died in 1876, although a few children of Tasmanian women by white fathers survived.

The Tasmanians were few in number, but their extermination was important in Australian history. Tasmania was the first Australian colony to solve its "native problem." Many whites on the Australian mainland wanted to imitate the Tasmanian solution, but they also learned a lesson from it. Because the Tasmanian genocide was carried out in full view of the urban press, it drew negative comments. The extermination of the much more numerous mainland Aborigines would occur on the frontier, far from urban centers.

The shooting and poisoning of Australian Aborigines continued long into the twentieth century. In 1928, for example, police massacred thirty-one Aborigines at Alice Springs. The mainland Aborigines were too numerous to exterminate completely, as had been done with the Tasmanians. But from the arrival of British colonists in 1788 to the census of 1921, the Aboriginal population fell from about three hundred thousand to sixty thousand.

Today, white Australians' attitudes toward their murderous past vary widely. Government policy and many people's private views have become more sympathetic to the Aborigines. Other whites, however, deny responsibility for the genocide.

scendants of the early settlers of
ia have been branded as the
of murderers who were respon-
the genocide of the Tasmanian
ne. Is this really true?

Encyclopaedia Britannica Re-

have never lived there. Calder said . . .
"the natives had much the better of the
warfare . . ."

They had developed remarkable skill
for surprise attacks. They would stealth-
ily creep up on an isolated farm and
surround it. After watching for hours,
sometimes days, they would take the occupants by surprise, massacre them and
burn their house and out-buildings.
Then, they would move on to some
pioneer family in another part of the
island and repeat the massacre.

A trick frequently employed by the
Tasmanian natives was to approach
isolated settlers, apparently unarmed.
They would wave their arms about in a

ing in Tasmania at the first white settlers' arrival in 1803 vary from 2000 to a
mere 700. Some reports claim 700
would be the absolute maximum at the
time of the first settlement and they
were, even then, fast dying out.

The factors which killed the Tasmanian Aborigines become apparent
after careful research. There were (1)
their eating habits (2) hazards of birth
(3) lack of hygiene (4) their marriage or
mating customs (5) dangerous "magic"
surgery (6) exposure to the harsh climate of Tasmania.

The eating habits of the Tasmanian
natives alone were enough to wipe them
out. It was their custom to eat everything that was available in one sitting

A LETTER WRITER DENIES GENOCIDE

IN 1982 *THE BULLETIN*, ONE OF AUSTRALIA'S
leading newspapers, printed a letter that shows how
some Australian whites could energetically deny that
genocide ever took place in their country. Patricia
Cobern, the woman who wrote the letter, claimed
that the peace-loving, moral settlers of Tasmania
had not exterminated the treacherous, murderous,
warlike, filthy native people. The Tasmanians had
died out because of their bad health practices,
such as never bathing, and also because they had a
death wish and lacked religious beliefs. It was just a
coincidence, Cobern implied, that after thousands
of years of existence, they happened to die out
during a conflict with the white settlers. The only
massacres were of settlers by Tasmanians, never the
other way around. Besides, according to Cobern, the
settlers armed themselves only in self-defense, were
unfamiliar with guns, and never shot more than forty-
one Tasmanians at one time.

265

Group Killing

Mass killings that can be considered genocides have occurred in many time periods and parts of the world. How exactly do we define *genocide*? It means "group killing." Victims are selected because they belong to a particular group, whether or not an individual victim has done something that might cause him or her to be killed. Groups have become targets of genocide because of:

* Race: One example is the killing of dark-skinned Tasmanians by white Australians.
* Nationality: In 1940, during World War II, Russians massacred Polish officers in the Katyn Forest.
* Ethnic differences: The Tutsi and Hutu, two black African peoples, slaughtered each other in the nations of Burundi and Rwanda in the 1970s and 1990s.
* Religion: Christians and Muslims, for example, have killed each other in the Middle Eastern nation of Lebanon and elsewhere.
* Politics: During the 1970s, the Khmer Rouge Party of Cambodia killed thousands of Cambodians.

Must killings be carried out by governments to be considered genocide, or do private acts also count? There is no clear answer. Some genocides have been well planned and entirely official, such as the killing of Jews, Gypsies, and other groups by the Nazi Party in Germany. Others have been private killings, as when land developers in Brazil hire professional hunters to exterminate native people. Many genocides involve both official and private killings. American Indians, for example, were killed by private citizens and the U.S. Army alike.

Another question concerns the cause of death. If people die in large numbers because of heartless actions that were not specifically designed to kill them, does that count as genocide? In another example from American history, President Andrew Jackson forced the Choctaw, Cherokee, and Creek Indians of the southeastern United States to move west of the Mississippi in the 1830s. Jackson did not deliberately plan for many Indians to die on the way because of lack of supplies and bitter winter weather, but he did not take the steps needed to keep them alive.

What reasons or motives lie behind genocidal killings? There are four types of motives, although some killings may be driven by more than one motive.

The most common motive may arise when a militarily stronger people tries to occupy the land of a weaker people, who resist. Examples include the extermination of the Tasmanians and Australian Aborigines, the American Indians, and the Araucanian people of Argentina.

Another common motive involves a long power struggle within a society that includes different groups. One group seeks a final end to the struggle by eliminating the other group. This was the case with history's largest known genocide: the killing of political opponents by the government of the Soviet Union, a former nation made up of Russia and a number of neighboring countries. The Soviet government killed sixty-six million of its own citizens between 1917 and 1959. An estimated twenty million died in a single ten-year period starting in 1929.

Those first two motives for genocide involve land and power. The third motive is scapegoating, in which members of a helpless minority are killed because they are blamed for the frustrations and fears of their killers. Jews were killed by fourteenth-century Christians as scapegoats for the bubonic plague. They were targeted again by Nazis during World War II as scapegoats for Germany's defeat in World War I.

Scapegoat killings may also involve the fourth type of genocide: racial or religious persecution. The Nazis' extermination of Jews and Gypsies was based in part on twisted ideas of "racial purity," while the list of religious massacres is long. Christian crusaders massacred the Muslims and Jews of Jerusalem in 1099, for example, and French Catholics massacred French Protestants in 1572. Racial and religious motives often contribute to genocides based on land and power struggles as well as those involving scapegoating.

Murder and War in the Animal World

Is man the only animal that kills members of his own species? Many writers and some scientists have thought so. The famed twentieth-century biologist Konrad Lorenz argued that animals' aggressive urges are held in check by instincts, or built-in behaviors, that keep them from murder. This balance became upset in human history when we invented weapons, because our instincts were no longer strong enough to hold back our new powers of killing.

But studies in recent years have documented murder in many, though certainly not all, animal species. Massacre of a neighboring individual or troop may benefit an animal, if the killer can then take over the neighbor's territory, food, or females. Attacks, however, also involve risk to the attacker, who might be injured or even killed. Looking at the potential costs and benefits of murder may explain why some species, but not others, kill their own.

Animals of nonsocial species are solitary. Murders in these species involve just one individual killing another. But in social species—such as lions, wolves, hyenas, and ants—murder may take the form of coordinated group attacks. Members of one troop attack a neighboring troop in a mass killing, or "war." The form of war varies among species. Attackers may drive off males, or kill them, sparing the females to mate with them. Sometimes, as with wolves, both males and females may be killed.

In seeking to understand the origins of genocide, we are especially interested in the behavior of our closest relatives, the chimpanzees and gorillas. Until the 1970s any biologist would have thought that humans' ability to use tools and plan together in groups made us far more murderous than apes—if apes were murderous at all. Discoveries since that time, however, suggest that a gorilla or chimpanzee is as likely as the average human to be murdered.

Among gorillas, males fight each other over harems of females, and the winner may kill the loser's infants as well as the loser himself. Such fighting is a major cause of death for infant and adult male gorillas. The typical gorilla mother loses at least one infant to a murderous male in the course of her life, and 38 percent of infant gorilla deaths are due to infanticide, or the murder of infants.

Chimpanzees are now known to commit murder and wage war. Jane Goodall, a pioneer in studying wild African chimpanzees, documented in detail the extermination of one band of chimps by another between 1974 and 1977. Groups of attackers, including some females, several times traveled into a neighboring troop's territory and ganged up on individual members of that troop. At least one female in the victim troop was killed along with several males. Other females were forced to join the attackers' troop. Similar long-term conflicts between groups have been observed for other troops of common chimpanzees, but none for bonobos.

Genocidal chimps appear to show signs of deliberate intention and basic planning—sneaking quickly, quietly, and nervously into another troop's territory, waiting in trees, and then swiftly attacking an "enemy" chimp. Chimpanzees also share with us the trait of xenophobia. They recognize members of other bands as different from their own band, and treat them very differently.

Of all our human hallmarks—art, spoken language, drug use, and more—genocide may be the one that comes to us most directly from our animal ancestors. Common chimps carry out planned killings, exterminations of neighboring bands, wars of territorial conquest, and kidnappings of females. This behavior suggests that one major reason for our human hallmark of group living was defense against other human groups, especially once we had acquired weapons and a large enough brain to plan ambushes. We may have been our own prey, and also the predator that forced us into group living.

A History of Genocide

Even if humans are not unique among animals in our murderous ways, could our murderous ways be a sick product of modern civilization? Some modern writers, disgusted by the destruction of "primitive" societies by "advanced" societies, think that hunter-gatherer or premodern societies are the human ideal. They paint a picture of people in such societies as peace-loving "noble savages" who, at worst, commit only isolated murders, not massacres.

Certainly some premodern societies seem less warlike than others. But when we look at early written history, records show that genocide occurred frequently. The wars of the Greeks and Trojans, the Romans and the people of the African colony of Carthage, and the Assyrians, Babylonians, and Persians ended with the slaughter of the defeated group, or perhaps with the killing of the men and the enslavement of the women. Most people know the biblical story of how the walls of Jericho came tumbling down at the sound of Joshua's trumpet. Not everyone remembers what happened next. Joshua obeyed the Lord's command to slaughter the inhabitants of Jericho and a number of other cities as well.

We find similar episodes in records of the wars of the crusaders, the Pacific islanders, and many other groups. Slaughter has not always followed defeat in war, of course. But it has happened often enough that it must be seen as more than a rare exception in our view of human nature. Between 1950 and the early 1990s alone, the world saw almost twenty episodes of genocide. Two of them claimed more than a million victims (Bangladesh in 1971, Cambodia in the late 1970s). Four others had more than 100,000 victims each. In 1994, for example, more than 800,000 people were killed in genocidal massacres in Rwanda. Genocidal warfare in the neighboring Democratic Republic of Congo has led to the deaths of at least 2.5 million people since 1998.

Genocide appears to have been part of our prehuman and human heritage for millions of years. In this long history, is there something different about modern genocides? There is no doubt that Joseph Stalin of the Soviet Union and

(right)
A child gazes at photographs in Cambodia's Tuol Sleng Museum of Genocide. Housed in a building that was first a school, then a prison and torture center, the museum commemorates the lives lost in the 1970s during the Cambodian genocide.

Adolf Hitler of Germany set new records for the number of victims. They had three advantages over killers of earlier centuries: denser population centers, improved communications for rounding up victims, and improved technology for mass killing.

It's harder to say whether technology makes genocide psychologically easier today. Biologist Konrad Lorenz argued that it does. He reasoned that as we evolved from apes, we depended more and more on cooperation between individuals. Societies could not survive unless humans developed strong inhibitions, or instinctive feelings, against killing other humans. Throughout most of our history, our weapons killed at close range, but modern push-button weapons have bypassed our inhibitions by letting us kill from a distance, without seeing our victims' faces. This has made it easier for us to stomach mass killings.

I'm uncertain about whether this psychological argument explains modern genocides. The past seems to have had just as frequent genocides as the present, even if the number of victims was smaller. To understand genocides further, we must consider the ethics—what we consider to be the rules of right and wrong—of killing.

Ethical Codes—and Why We Break Them

Our urge to kill is almost always held back by our ethics, our understanding that something (in this case, murder) is wrong, or immoral. The puzzle is: What unleashes the urge to kill?

One key is that we evolved to think in terms of "us" and "them." Like chimpanzees, gorillas, and social carnivores such as lions and wolves, early humans lived in bands, each with its own territory. The world was smaller and simpler then. Every "us" knew only a few types of "them," our immediate neighbors. That remained true for some human groups into modern times.

In New Guinea, for example, each tribe kept up a shifting network of alliance and war with its closest neighbors. A person might enter the next valley on a friendly visit (never completely without danger) or on a war raid, but there was little chance of being able to travel through a series of several valleys in friendship. The powerful rules about treatment of one's fellow "us" did not apply to "them," those dimly understood, neighboring enemies.

As the world grew larger and more complex for some societies, this tribal territorialism remained. Writings from ancient Greece show that the Greeks saw themselves as "us" and everyone else as "them." The ideal was not to treat all people equally, but to reward one's friends and punish one's enemies. Just like hyena bands or chimpanzee troops, human groups practiced a double standard of behavior. There were strong inhibitions about killing one of "us," but a green light to kill "them" when it was safe to do so.

Over time, this ancient double standard has become less acceptable as an ethical code. There has been a tendency toward a more universal code of behavior—one that calls for treating people more equally, toward having similar rules for interacting with different peoples. Genocide conflicts directly with a universal ethical code. So how do people who commit genocide wiggle out of the conflict between their actions and the universal code of ethics that has come to be the modern ideal? Simple. They blame the victim, using one or more of three justifications.

First, most believers in a universal ethical code still believe it is all right to defend themselves. This is useful because "they" can usually be tricked or driven into some behavior that calls for "our" self-defense. Even Hitler claimed self-defense when he started World War II. He went to the trouble of faking a Polish attack on a German border post.

Second, having the "right" religion or race or political belief, or claiming to represent progress or a higher level of civilization, is a traditional justification for doing anything, including genocide, to people on the "wrong" side or with the "wrong" belief.

Finally, our ethical codes regard humans and animals differently. Those who commit genocide in the modern world routinely compare their victims to animals in order to justify the killings. Nazis considered Jews to be subhuman lice. French settlers in Algeria called the local Muslims rats. Boers (white descendants of Dutch settlers in South Africa) referred to black Africans as baboons.

Americans have used all three of these excuses to justify their treatment of the American Indian. Because we claim to believe in a universal code of ethics, our traditional attitudes and stories about the genocide say that whites killed Indians in self-defense, that white civilization was superior and destined to keep advancing across the land, and that the victims were savage animals.

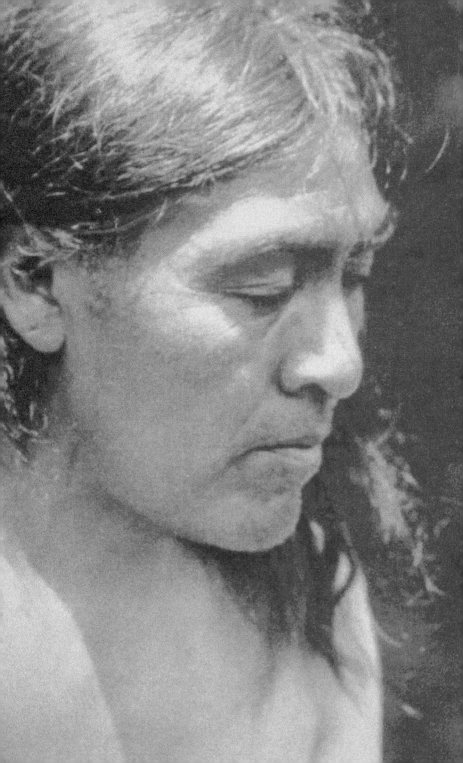

THE LAST OF HIS TRIBE

ON AUGUST 29, 1911, A STARVING, TERRIFIED Indian named Ishi emerged from a remote canyon in Northern California, where he had been hiding for forty-one years. Ishi was the last survivor of a genocide—the extermination of his people, the Yahi tribe.

Most of the Yahis were massacred by settlers between 1853 and 1870. Sixteen people survived the final massacre in 1870. They went into hiding in the Mount Lassen wilderness and continued to live as hunter-gatherers. By 1908 their number had dwindled to four. That year, surveyors stumbled on their camp and took all their tools, clothes, and winter food supply. As a result, three of the Yahis—Ishi's mother, his sister, and an old man—died. Ishi remained alone for three more years until he could stand it no longer. He walked out to white civilization, expecting to be killed. Instead, he was employed by the University of California Museum in San Francisco. He died of tuberculosis in 1916.

Ishi was not just the last member of the Yahi people. He was also known as the last "wild" Indian in the United States. Fifteen years after his death, the white killers of his tribe were still publishing their accounts of the genocide. Today, however, Ishi is remembered as a survivor who, after joining white society, shared his story and his knowledge of Indian language and crafts.

(*left*)
Ishi, who died in 1916, was the sole survivor of an American genocide—the extermination of his people, the Yahi Indians.

Looking to the Future

What genocides can we expect from *Homo sapiens* in the future? Plenty of trouble spots in the world seem ripe for genocide. Modern weapons permit one person to kill ever larger numbers of victims, far from the battlefield. It is even imaginable that someone could commit universal genocide, killing the entire human race.

At the same time, I see reasons to hope that the future may not be as murderous as the past. In many countries today, people of different races or religions or ethnic groups live together, with varying degrees of social justice but at least without open mass murder. Some genocides have been interrupted, reduced, or prevented by third parties who intervened to keep the peace.

Another hopeful sign is that travel, TV, photography, and the Internet let us see people who live ten thousand miles away as human, like us. Technology is blurring the line between "us" and "them" that makes genocide possible. While genocide was considered acceptable or even admirable in the world before first contact, the modern spread of international culture and our knowledge about distant peoples make genocide ever harder to justify.

But the potential for genocide lies within all of us. As world population grows, conflicts between societies and within them will sharpen. Humans will have more urge to kill one another, and better weapons with which to do it. To listen to stories of genocide is unbearably painful. But if we turn away and do not try to understand this destructive part of human nature, when will it be our turn to become the killers, or the victims?

The ruins of Pueblo Bunito, the largest structure in Chaco Canyon. This one-time Anasazi settlement is now Chaco Culture National Historical Park in New Mexico.

PART FIVE

REVERSING
OUR PROGRESS
OVERNIGHT

OUR SPECIES NOW COVERS THE EARTH AND commands a larger share of the planet's productivity than ever before. That's the good news. The bad news is that, as the next three chapters will show, we are now reversing our progress much more rapidly than we created it. Our power threatens our own existence. Will we suddenly blow ourselves up, or sink slowly into a stew of global warming, pollution, more mouths to feed with less food, and the loss of species we need to survive? And are these dangers really new ones that arose only after the Industrial Revolution of the late eighteenth and nineteenth centuries?

Most people believe that Nature exists in a state of balance: predators don't exterminate their prey; grazing animals don't overgraze their food sources. In this view, humans are the only misfits. If this were true, Nature would hold no lessons for us, because animals and their environments would never get out of balance.

It's true that species don't naturally become extinct as rapidly as we are now exterminating them, except under rare circumstances—such as the mass die-off sixty-five million years ago, possibly due to an asteroid crashing to earth, that finished the dinosaurs. Still, Nature offers many examples of species exterminating other species. This usually happens when a predator is introduced to a new environment, where it meets prey species that are not used to it. After exterminating some of these species, the predator survives by switching to others.

Rats, cats, goats, pigs, ants, and even snakes have become killers when they have been carried by humans to new environments. One example is a tree snake native to Australia. During World War II it was accidentally carried on ships or planes to the Pacific island of Guam, which had no snakes. By now the Australian tree snake has wiped out or brought to the brink of extinction most of Guam's forest bird species, which had no chance to evolve behavior that would defend against snakes.

We humans are the prime example of a switching predator, one that can switch to new prey when one type of prey becomes scarce or extinct. We eat everything from snails and seaweed to whales, mushrooms, and strawberries. If we overharvest a species to the point of extinction, we just switch to another food source. For this reason, a wave of extinctions has followed us every time we have moved into an unoccupied part of the globe. Hawaiian bird species died out in great numbers after Polynesians reached Hawaii fifteen hundred years ago, for example.

What about animals? Do they ever destroy their own resource base? It doesn't happen often, because animal populations tend to rise and fall along with their food supply. Still, some animal populations have eaten themselves out of food, and perished. In 1944, twenty-nine reindeer were introduced to St. Matthew Island in the Bering Sea. By 1963 they had multiplied to six thousand. But reindeer eat slow-growing lichens, and on the small island these plants had no chance to recover from reindeer grazing, because the animals had nowhere to migrate. When a harsh winter struck, all the reindeer died except forty-one females and one sterile male, leaving a doomed population on an island littered with skeletons.

Ecological suicide by animals happens when populations suddenly become free of the forces that usually control their numbers. Humans have recently escaped from the former controls on our numbers. We eliminated predation on us long ago. Modern medicine has greatly reduced the number of deaths from infectious disease. Behaviors that used to limit population size, such as killing our offspring and waging near-permanent war, have become socially unacceptable. Our population continues to grow, but the example of the St. Matthew reindeer teaches us that no population can grow indefinitely.

Our present condition can be compared to events in the animal world. Like many switching predators, we eliminate some prey species when we colonize a new environment or gain new destructive power. Like some animal populations that escape their growth limits, we risk destroying ourselves by destroying our resource base.

What about the view that humans lived in a state of ecological balance before the Industrial Revolution, and that only in modern times have we exterminated species and overused our environment? The remaining chapters examine this idea. We will look first at the belief in a golden age when humans supposedly lived in harmony with nature. Then we'll look more closely at one of the biggest, most dramatic, and most controversial mass extinctions: the disappearance of many large mammals from the Americas, just as humans arrived. Finally, we'll try to determine how many species we have already driven to extinction, and what that might mean for our own future.

CHAPTER 14

THE GOLDEN AGE THAT NEVER WAS

WHEN EUROPEANS BEGAN TO SETTLE THE Americas, the air and rivers were pure, the landscape was green, and the Great Plains teemed with bison. Today we breathe smog, worry about toxic chemicals in our drinking water, pave over the landscape, and rarely see a large wild animal. Things are sure to get worse as more species go extinct and the pollution of our air and seas continues.

Two simple reasons go a long way toward explaining our worsening mess. One is that modern technology has far more power to cause havoc than the simple stone axes of the past. The other is that far more people are alive now than ever before. But there may be a third factor: a change in attitudes. Unlike modern city-dwellers, people who live outside industrial economies depend on their local environment for survival, and at least some of them understand and revere it. A New Guinea tribesman once explained to me, "It's our custom that if a hunter one day kills a pigeon in one direction from the village, he waits a week before hunting for pigeons again, and then goes in the opposite direction." We're only beginning to realize that many so-called primitive peoples practice sound conservation policies.

Environmentalists who are sickened by the damage that industrial societies are doing to the world often look to the past as a Golden Age, when everyone lived like those New Guinea tribesmen, in harmonious balance with the natural world. Until recently, I and many of my environmentalist colleagues shared this nostalgic view. That's why recent discoveries by archaeologists and paleontologists have come as something of a shock. It's now clear that preindustrial societies have been exterminating species, destroying habitats, and undermining their own existence for thousands of years.

If these discoveries are correct, can we use them as case histories to predict our own fate? Can these recent findings explain some mysterious collapses of ancient civilizations, such as those of Easter Island or the Maya?

New Zealand Minus Moas

New Zealand is a Pacific Ocean island country east of Australia. When British colonists began settling there in the nineteenth century, they found no native land mammals except bats. They did, though, find the bones and eggshells of large birds. These birds had already become extinct, but the Maori people—Polynesians who had settled New Zealand centuries earlier—called them moa.

Moas were ostrich-like birds. The largest species were ten feet tall and weighed up to five hundred pounds. Moas fed on twigs and leaves, making them New Zealand's bird version of plant-eating mammals such as deer and antelope. Other bird species had disappeared before Europeans arrived. Some were big and flightless, including a large duck and an enormous goose. These flightless birds were descended from birds that had flown to New

Zealand and then evolved to lose their wings. (They did not need wings because there were no humans or other mammal predators in New Zealand to hunt them.) Other little animals native to New Zealand had also become extinct or almost extinct, including frogs, snails, giant crickets, and strange mouselike bats that rolled up their wings and ran.

Fossils show that moas had survived on New Zealand for millions of years. Why did they finally become extinct? And when? Were the moas and other native creatures still alive when the ancestors of the Maoris arrived around 1000 AD?

When I first visited New Zealand, in 1966, people believed that the moas had died out because of a change in the climate. Any that had been alive when the first Maoris showed up must have been on their last legs. The Maoris were believed to be conservationists who could not have exterminated the moas. But three sets of discoveries overturned this idea.

First, the Ice Age ended in New Zealand around ten thousand years ago. After that, the climate was more favorable to moas. The last moas died full of food and enjoying the best climate they had seen for thousands of years.

Second, bird bones from Maori archaeological sites have been dated. They prove that all known moa species were abundant when the first Maoris stepped ashore. So were many other bird species now known only from fossil bones. Within a few centuries, they were extinct. It would be an incredible coincidence if dozens of species occupied New Zealand for millions of years and then happened to die out just when humans arrived.

Third, more than a hundred large archaeological sites are known where Maoris cut up large numbers of moas, cooked them in earth ovens, and threw out the remains. They ate the meat, used the skins for clothing, made fishhooks and jewelry from the bones, and blew the contents out of eggs to use the shells for carrying water. The vast number of moa skeletons says that the Maoris were slaughtering these big birds for many generations.

It is now clear that the Maoris exterminated moas, partly by killing them, partly by robbing their nests of eggs, and probably also by killing some of the forest in which the moas lived. Other bird species were exterminated as well.

What about New Zealand's smaller creatures— the crickets, snails, and bats? Deforestation may be part of the reason they went extinct, but the main reason was the other hunter the Maoris accidentally brought with them: rats! Just as moas evolved without humans and had no defenses against them, small creatures that had evolved in a rat-free environment were defenseless against these rodents.

When the first Maoris landed, they found a New Zealand full of creatures so strange that we would think they were science-fiction fantasies if we did not have their fossilized bones. It was like reaching another planet on which life had evolved. Within a short time, much of New Zealand's biological community had collapsed. Some of what remained died out in a second collapse following the arrival of Europeans. Today New Zealand has about half the bird species that greeted the Maoris, and many of the survivors are either at risk of extinction or limited to islands with few mammal pests. A few centuries of hunting had ended millions of years of moa history.

Madagascar's Vanished Giants
Polynesians were not the only prehistoric exterminators. Halfway around the world from

New Zealand is the world's fourth-largest island, Madagascar, off the coast of Africa. Its people, the Malagasy, are descended from seafaring Indonesians who crossed the Indian Ocean to trade with East Africa and settled the island between one and two thousand years ago.

Madagascar is home to many species found nowhere else, including two dozen species of small, monkey-like primates called lemurs. Littering Madagascar's beaches are eggshells the size of soccer balls, proof of vanished giant birds. The eggs were laid by half a dozen species of extinct flightless birds up to ten feet tall. Similar to ostriches and moas but more massive, these extinct creatures are now called elephant birds. Fossil bones show that Madagascar also once had a number of vanished large mammals and reptiles. Among them were giant tortoises, lemurs as large as gorillas, and a hippopotamus the size of a cow.

The bones of all these extinct species are known from fossil sites only a few thousand years old. Since they evolved and survived for millions of years before then, it is unlikely that all these extinct animals gave up the ghost just before hungry humans showed up. In fact, the elephant birds may have hung on long enough to become known to Arab traders, giving rise to the giant bird called the roc in the tale of Sindbad the Sailor.

Certainly some if not all of Madagascar's vanished giants were exterminated by the activities of the early Malagasy. Unintended actions, though, probably killed more big animals than hunters did. Fires that humans started to kill forest for pasture would have destroyed the animals' habitats, as would the grazing of cattle and goats. Dogs and pigs introduced by humans would have preyed on ground-dwelling animals, their young, and their eggs. By the time Portuguese explorers arrived around 1500, Madagascar's once-abundant elephant birds had been reduced to eggshells covering the beaches, skeletons in the ground, and vague memories of rocs.

The Easter Island Question

The so-called Golden Age was tarnished by more than the extermination of species. Early human societies also destroyed habitats. One dramatic example is Easter Island, which lies in the Pacific about 2,300 miles west of the South American nation of Chile.

An aura of mystery has clung to Easter Island ever since it and its Polynesian inhabitants were "discovered" by a Dutch explorer in 1722. There, on one of the world's most isolated scraps of land, people had carved hundreds of statues out of volcanic rock. The statues weighed up to eighty-five tons and measured as much as thirty-seven feet in height. Without metal or wheels, using no power source except human muscle, the islanders had carried many of these statues to platforms several miles from where the stone was quarried. Other statues had been left unfinished or abandoned, as if the carvers and movers had suddenly walked off their jobs. Many statues were still standing when the Dutch explorer arrived, but by 1840 the islanders had pushed them all over. How were these huge statues made and moved? Why did the islanders stop carving them and eventually topple them over?

To answer the first question, living Easter Islanders showed twentieth-century researcher Thor Heyerdahl how their ancestors used log rollers to move the statues. The answer to the second question lies in the island's grim history, revealed by archaeological and paleontological research. When Polynesians settled Easter Island around 400 AD, the island was covered by forest, which the settlers gradually cleared, for timber and to plant gardens. By around 1500 the human population had grown to about 7,000. The islanders had carved about a thousand statues and raised at least 324 of them.

But the forest had been destroyed so completely that not a single tree survived.

Carving stopped because the islanders no longer had the logs needed to move and raise the statues. But deforestation also brought starvation. Without trees, the soil eroded, and gardens became less productive. Without trees, the islanders could not build canoes for fishing. Island society collapsed in a holocaust of war and cannibalism, scattering spear points across the land. Rival clans pulled down each other's statues, and people lived in caves for self-protection. What had once been a lush island supporting a remarkable civilization became the Easter Island of today: a barren grassland littered with fallen statues, supporting less than a third of its former population.

(right)
Enormous statues gaze out over the wastes of Easter Island, where a once-thriving culture collapsed after the islanders cut down the forests.

"MYSTERY ISLANDS" OF THE PACIFIC

HENDERSON ISLAND IS AN EXTREMELY REMOTE speck of land in the tropical Pacific Ocean. Made of jungle-covered coral, riddled with crevices, it is totally unsuited for agriculture. It has been uninhabited ever since Europeans first saw it in 1606. That's why it was a big surprise when paleontologists identified the bones of three species of pigeons and three species of seabirds that had gone extinct on Henderson between five hundred and eight hundred years ago. Fossils of the same six species, or their close relatives, had already been found on islands inhabited by Polynesians, where it was clear how they could have been exterminated by people. But how could they have gone extinct on uninhabited Henderson?

The mystery was solved by the discovery of archaeological sites on Henderson, proving that Polynesians had lived there for several hundred years

before Europeans ever saw the island. These islanders lived on pigeons, seabirds, and fish, until they wiped out the bird populations. With their food supply destroyed or greatly reduced, they either starved to death or abandoned the island. The Pacific contains at least eleven other "mystery islands" besides Henderson. These islands were found uninhabited by Europeans, but archaeological evidence shows that Polynesians had formerly lived there—sometimes for several centuries. All these islands were small or poorly suited to farming. Their inhabitants depended on birds and other animals for food.

We know that early Polynesians overused and exterminated birds and wild animals in Hawaii and other islands where they lived for long periods. If they did the same thing on the small "mystery islands," these specks in the ocean may represent the graveyards of human populations that destroyed their own resource base.

Islands and Continents

Polynesia and Madagascar are examples of the waves of extinction that probably washed over all large islands after the first human settlers arrived. Islands where life evolved without humans used to have unique species of big animals that modern zoologists never saw alive. Mediterranean islands such as Crete and Cyprus had pygmy hippos and giant tortoises, dwarf elephants and dwarf deer. The West Indies lost ground sloths, a bear-sized rodent, and owls of several sizes: normal, giant, colossal, and titanic. Small creatures such as lizards, frogs, snails, and birds disappeared, too—thousands of species lost, when you add up all the islands in the oceans.

Paleontologist Storrs Olson has called these island extinctions "one of the swiftest and most profound biological catastrophes in the history of the world." We won't be sure that humans were responsible for all of it until the bones of the last animals and the remains of the first people have been dated more exactly for every island, as has already been done for Polynesia and Madagascar.

The continents may have seen their own extinction waves, but in the more distant past.

About eleven thousand years ago, around the likely time that the first ancestors of the American Indians reached the Americas, most large mammals became extinct throughout North and South America. Debate has raged over whether these species were done in by Indian hunters or just happened to perish by climate change around the same time. In the next chapter, I'll explain why I think hunters did it. But it is much harder to pinpoint dates and causes for events that happened around eleven thousand years ago than it is for recent events, such as the moa-versus-Maori collision within the past thousand years. Within the past fifty thousand years, for example, Australia was colonized by the ancestors of today's Aborigines *and* lost most of its species of big animals. We do not yet know if the arrival of humans caused the extinctions.

We can be fairly sure that the first people to reach islands created disaster for island species. The jury is still out, though, on the question of whether this also happened on continents.

Anasazi Apocalypse

Our second case of habitat destruction before the modern industrial era involves one of the most advanced Indian civilizations in North America. When Spanish explorers reached what is today the U.S. Southwest, they found gigantic multistory dwellings called pueblos standing empty in the middle of treeless desert. One of them, the 650-room pueblo at Chaco Culture National Historical Park in New Mexico, was five stories high, 670 feet long, and 315 feet wide. It was the largest structure ever built in North America until the steel skyscrapers of the late nineteenth century. The Navajo who lived in the area knew of the vanished builders only as Anasazi, meaning "the Ancient Ones."

The building of the Chaco pueblos started soon after 900 AD. Sometime in the twelfth century, just two hundred years later, people stopped living in them. Why did the Anasazi erect a city in a barren wasteland? Where did they get their firewood and the two hundred thousand wooden beams that supported their roofs? And why did they abandon the city?

The usual view was that the Anasazi abandoned Chaco Canyon because of a drought. A different story, though, is told by the plants of Chaco, and how they changed over time. Paleobotanists are scientists who study plant remains from the past. When they examined plant remains from around Chaco, they learned that when the pueblos were built, they were not surrounded by desert. Instead, they stood in the middle of a woodland of short pinyon and juniper trees, with a forest of taller ponderosa pine trees nearby. This was the source of the Anasazi firewood and timber.

As people continued to live at Chaco, however, the woodland and forest were cleared until the environment became the treeless wasteland it remains today. People had to go at least ten miles for firewood, and much farther to find timber big enough for building. They made an elaborate road system to haul spruce and fir logs from mountains more than fifty miles away, using only their own muscle power.

The deforestation around the pueblos caused increasing soil erosion and water runoff. The irrigation channels that the Anasazi dug to bring water to their fields carved out deeper and deeper gullies, until, at last, the groundwater may have dropped below the level of the fields, making it impossible to channel water into them. Without irrigation, the Anasazi couldn't grow crops. Drought may have contributed to the Anasazi abandonment of Chaco Canyon, but a self-inflicted ecological disaster was another factor.

Ecological Collapse in the Cradle of Civilization
Another ecological collapse—this time around the city of Petra, in the Middle Eastern kingdom of Jordan—sheds light on why the power center of ancient civilization kept shifting. Many crucial developments in human culture arose in the Middle East, including agriculture, animal domestication, writing, imperial states, and battle chariots. With the overthrow of Persia (now Iran) by Alexander the Great, the center of power in the ancient world shifted from the Middle East to Greece. Later it shifted again, to Rome, and later again, to western and northern Europe. Why did each powerful region or state eventually lose its position at the center?

One good theory is that each ancient center of civilization in turn ruined its resource base. The Middle East and the lands around the Mediterranean Sea were not always the dry, barren, overused landscape that appears today. In ancient times much of the area was a lush mosaic of wooded hills and fertile valleys. Human populations cut forests, cleared steep slopes for farming, overgrazed too many livestock, and planted crops too close together for the soil to recover. The result each time was soil erosion, flooding, crop failure, and the collapse of local human society.

This view of ancient environmental destruction is supported by both ancient writings and modern archaeology. One example is Petra, a "lost city" carved in rock—and known to movie fans because part of *Indiana Jones and the Last Crusade* was filmed there.

Petra was clearly a wealthy and powerful city. It flourished for hundreds of years as a trade center and was well known in Roman times. How did it support itself in a bleak desert landscape, and why was it abandoned and forgotten? Paleobotanists studying pollen and other preserved plant materials have learned that Petra once stood in a woodland. As in Chaco Canyon, residents gathered firewood and cut timber. They also grazed goats, which ate small trees. Pollen grains from 900 AD show that by that time two-thirds of the trees had disappeared. Even shrubs and grasses had declined. The ravaged land surrounding Petra could no longer support a major city.

Petra is just one of many ancient cities around the world that stand today as monuments to states that destroyed their means of survival. Whole civilizations, such as the Maya of Central America and the Harappan culture of India and Pakistan, may have collapsed because their growing populations overwhelmed their environments. History books often dwell on kings and barbarian invasions, but in the long run, deforestation and erosion may have done more to shape the course of human history.

ANSWERS IN MIDDENS

BY STUDYING CENTURIES-OLD PLANT REMAINS, paleobotanists gained a picture of the changing types of plants that grew around Chaco Canyon and Petra over long periods of time. This is how we know that forested areas changed to shrubland, then desert. But how did the scientists get ahold of centuries-old pollen and plant fibers? They relied on small plant-eating animals that gather vegetation and store it in underground shelters called middens.

Little rodents called pack rats were the midden builders of Chaco Canyon. Although each pack rat midden is usually abandoned after fifty or a hundred years of use, bits of vegetation stored by generations of pack rats remain behind. In dry desert conditions, those bits of plant material remain well preserved for centuries. Scientists can use radiocarbon techniques to date each

Petra, an ancient city in the country of Jordan.

midden, which is like a time capsule, preserving samples of the local vegetation from the time the midden was in use.

Petra never had pack rats, but it does have middens. Rabbit-size mammals called hyraxes live in the Middle East. Like pack rats, hyraxes store their food (plant materials) in underground middens. Old hyrax middens at Petra contained samples of up to a hundred different plant species. These samples told scientists what type of habitat existed when each midden was being used by animals that lived at the same time as ancient civilizations. Animal middens turned out to be a valuable source of information about the history of both habitats and humans.

Environmentalism Past and Future

The supposed golden age of environmentalism looks more and more like a myth. But we do know that some modern people who live outside industrial society practice good conservation. We also know that not all species have been exterminated, and not all habitats have been destroyed, so the golden age couldn't have been all dark.

Small, long-established societies where everyone is more or less equal tend to evolve conservationist practices. They've had plenty of time to get to know their local environment and to see how it's in their best interest to take care of it. Damage is more likely to occur when people suddenly colonize an unfamiliar environment, as the Maoris and the Easter Islanders did, or when they advance along a frontier, which lets them simply move on to a new environment when they've destroyed the one behind them.

Damage also occurs when people acquire a new technology with destructive powers they haven't had time to understand—this is happening now in New Guinea, where pigeon populations are being devastated by shotguns. Damage is also likely in big centralized states where power is concentrated in the hands of rulers who are out of touch with their environment. Finally, some species and habitats are more vulnerable to damage than others. Flightless birds with no fear of humans were easy prey. Dry, fragile environments such as the American Southwest and the Mediterranean Sea region were easily degraded.

What practical lessons can we learn from knowing how earlier people wiped out species and ruined resources? Government planners might be guided by the past. The American Southwest has more than one hundred thousand acres of pinyon-juniper woodland that we are using more and more for firewood. Unfortunately, the U.S. Forest Service has little information to help it decide how much wood can be taken without destroying the woodland. Yet the Anasazi already tried the experiment, and it failed. Woodland still hasn't recovered in Chaco Canyon after more than eight hundred years. Paying archaeologists to determine how much firewood the Anasazi consumed would be cheaper than making the same mistake and ruining a hundred thousand acres of woodland, as we may now be doing.

It's always been hard for humans to know the rate at which they can harvest biological resources for a long time without using them up. By the time the signs of decline are clear enough to convince everyone, it may be too late to save the species or habitat in question. The Maoris who consumed New Zealand's moas and the Anasazi who killed off pinyon-juniper woodland were not guilty of moral failure. Instead, they failed to solve a really difficult ecological problem.

There are two big differences between us and those involved in the tragic ecological failures of the past. We have scientific knowledge that they lacked, and we have the means to communicate and share what we know. We can read all about the ecological disasters of the past. Yet we continue to hunt whales and clear tropical rain forest as if no one had ever hunted moas or cleared pinyon-juniper woodland. If the past was a golden age of ignorance, the present is an iron age of willful blindness.

CHAPTER 15

BLITZKRIEG AND THANKSGIVING IN THE NEW WORLD

THE UNITED STATES DEVOTES TWO NATIONAL holidays, Columbus Day and Thanksgiving, to celebrating the European "discovery" of America. No holidays celebrate the much earlier discovery of the Americas by the ancestors of the Indians. Yet archaeology suggests that, for sheer drama, the earlier discovery dwarfs the adventures of Christopher Columbus and the Pilgrims of Plymouth Rock. Within perhaps no more than a thousand years, Indians found a way through an Arctic ice sheet and swept all the way to Patagonia, at the southern tip of South America. At the end of that time they had populated two productive and unexplored continents.

(*left*)
Standing more than twelve feet tall, this Columbian mammoth skeleton may be the largest in the world. Until it became extinct around 10,000 years ago, this species roamed the plains of North America—and was hunted by the early human inhabitants of the continent, who used spears to bring down mammoths and other big game.

The Indians' march southward was the greatest expansion of our species' range in the history of *Homo sapiens*. Nothing like it can ever happen again. It was marked by another drama: a mass extinction. When the first hunters arrived, they found the Americas teeming with big mammals that are now extinct: elephant-like mammoths and mastodons, three-ton ground sloths, beavers the size of bears, and sabertoothed cats, plus lions, cheetahs, camels, horses, and more.

What happened when humans met these beasts? Archaeologists and paleontologists disagree. The interpretation that makes the most sense to me is a "blitzkrieg"—a lightning-fast assault in which the animals were quickly exterminated by humans, perhaps in just ten years at any given site. If that view is correct, it would have been the quickest and most severe extinction of big animals since the dinosaurs disappeared. It would also have been the first of many blitzkriegs that marred our mythical golden age of environmental innocence.

The Greatest Expansion in Human History

The confrontation between animals and the first people in the Americas was the last act in a long epic of human expansion. Spreading out of their center of origins in Africa, humans expanded into Asia and Europe, and then from Asia to Australia. This left North and South America as the last habitable continents without people. So how and when did people get to the Americas?

From Canada to the southern tip of South America, Indians look more like one another than the inhabitants of any other continent. They must have arrived here too recently to have evolved much genetic diversity. At the same time, American Indians resemble certain East Asian peoples. The evidence from both archaeology and genetics proves that Native Americans originated from Asia. The easiest route from Asia to America is across the Bering Strait, a narrow strip of water that separates Siberia and Alaska. Between twenty-five thousand and ten thousand years ago, during the Ice Age, sea levels were lower all over the world because so much water was locked up in ice. At that time, Siberia was linked to Alaska by a land bridge that is now under the Bering Strait.

Colonizing the Americas needed more than a land bridge. It also needed people to be living at the Asian end of the land bridge, in Siberia.

Because of its harsh climate, the Siberian Arctic was not colonized until late in human history. But by twenty thousand years ago, mammoth hunters were living there, leaving stone tools and other traces of their presence. And stone tools similar to those of the Siberian hunters have been found in Alaska, dating from around twelve thousand years ago.

Once they had reached present-day Alaska, the Ice Age hunters found themselves separated from what is now the United States by another barrier. A broad ice cap stretched across Canada. Then, around twelve thousand years ago, a narrow, ice-free corridor opened up just east of the Rocky Mountains. We know that hunters soon moved south through that ice-free corridor, because their stone tools have turned up in archaeological sites south of the ice cap. At that point the hunters met America's great beasts, and the drama began.

Archaeologists call these pioneering ancestral Indians the Clovis people because their stone tools were first recognized at a site near Clovis, New Mexico. Since then, Clovis tools or ones similar to them have been found throughout North America. These tools are much like the ones used by earlier eastern European and Siberian hunters, but with the addition of grooves on both sides of the stone spear points. These grooves made it easier to tie the stone points to sticks, but we don't know whether the hunters threw their weapons or stabbed with them. Somehow, though, the hunters drove the points into big mammals hard enough to penetrate bone. Scientists have dug up mammoth and bison skeletons with Clovis points inside them.

The Clovis people spread quickly. The known sites in the United States were occupied for just a few centuries, just before eleven thousand years ago. Then Clovis points were replaced by smaller, more finely made tools called Folsom points. (These were discovered near Folsom, New Mexico.) These points are found with bison bones but never with mammoth bones.

Why did hunters switch from the Clovis spear points to the smaller Folsom points? Maybe they no longer needed the big points, because the biggest game animals were gone. There were no mammoths left. Camels, horses, giant ground sloths, and other big mammals had disappeared as well. Both North and South

SPECIES EXTINCTION AND HUMAN POPULATION

Graph source: USGS

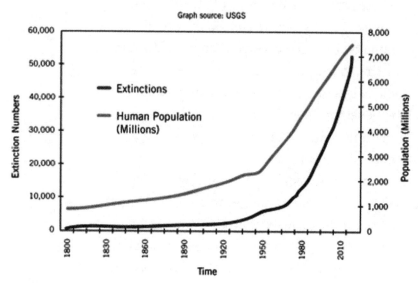

As the human population has grown since 1800 (measured on the right), the number of species becoming extinct has steadily increased (shown on the left). The parallel lines raise the question: How many of these modern extinctions have humans caused?

America lost large numbers of big mammal species at the same time.

Many paleontologists blame the extinctions on climate and habitat change at the end of the Ice Age. Yet the end of the Ice Age brought more habitat for animals, not less, as melting ice opened up areas of forest and grassland. Anyway, the big American mammals had already survived the ends of at least twenty-two earlier ice ages. In addition, both warmth-loving *and* cold-loving species went extinct, which should not have been the case if the cause was climate change.

Paul Martin of the University of Arizona described the outcome of hunter-meets-mammals as a blitzkrieg. In his view, the first hunters to emerge from the ice-free corridor thrived and multiplied because they found an abundance of big-game animals that had no fear of humans and were easy to hunt. When game was killed off in one area, the hunters and their offspring fanned out into new areas and killed the mammal populations there. By the time the hunters had reached southern South America, most big mammal species of the Americas had been exterminated.

First in the Americas

Martin's blitzkrieg theory has drawn vigorous criticism. Doubters ask: Could a small band of hunters passing through the ice-free corridor breed fast enough to populate two continents in a thousand years? Could they cover the eight thousand miles to southern South America in that time? Were Clovis hunters really the first people in the Americas? And could they have killed millions of big animals so efficiently that not a single individual of many species survived?

In modern times, when colonists have settled an uninhabited island, their population has grown as rapidly as 3.4 percent a year. This growth rate—four children per couple, and a new generation every twenty years—would multiply 100 hunters into 10 million in only 340 years. To reach the tip of South America in 1,000 years, humans would have had to expand southward an average distance of 8 miles a year, an easy task. Some migrations of Africa's Zulu people in the nineteenth century are known to have covered 3,000 miles in 50 years.

As for whether the Clovis people were the first humans to spread south of the Canadian ice sheet, that's a harder question. It's also extremely controversial among archaeologists. Dozens of sites have been believed by a few researchers to contain evidence of human remains earlier than the Clovis people, but none of these supposed pre-Clovis sites is accepted without question by the whole scientific community.

In contrast, the evidence for the Clovis culture is undeniable, found in many places, and widely accepted. At site after site, archaeologists find a layer of Clovis tools with the bones of large extinct species. Above the Clovis layer is a younger layer of Folsom tools, but no bones of large mammals except bison. Below the Clovis layer lie thousands of years' worth of fossils of large extinct mammals, but no human tools or remains. It makes good sense to me that the Clovis people were the first Americans.

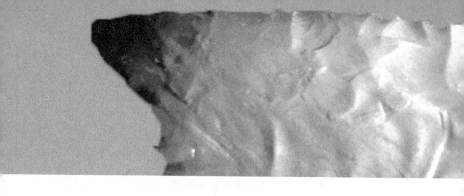

MEADOWCROFT AND MONTE VERDE: UNANSWERED QUESTIONS

SOME ARCHAEOLOGISTS CLAIM TO HAVE FOUND evidence of human presence in the Americas before the time of the Clovis people. Almost all these claims raise questions about whether the material used for radiocarbon dating was mixed with older material, whether the dated material was actually found with human remains, or whether tools supposedly made by humans are really just naturally shaped rocks.

The two most nearly convincing of the claimed "pre-Clovis" sites are Meadowcroft Rockshelter in Pennsylvania, dated to about sixteen thousand

years ago, and Monte Verde in Chile, South America, dated to at least thirteen thousand years ago. Monte Verde has many types of well-preserved human artifacts, but the radiocarbon dating of these artifacts is open to question. At Meadowcroft there has been debate about whether the radiocarbon dates are accurate, especially because plant and animal species from the site are not thought to have lived there until much more recently than sixteen thousand years ago. Until questions about Monte Verde and Meadowcroft can be answered with more certainty, the Clovis people should be considered the oldest definitely known inhabitants of the Americas.

A Clovis point on display at the Natural History Museum of Utah, Salt Lake City, Utah.

Exterminating the Mammoths

Another hotly debated argument about the blitzkrieg theory concerns the overhunting and extermination of big mammals. It seems hard to imagine Stone Age hunters killing mammoths at all, much less hunting them to extinction. Yet we know that Stone Age hunters who lived in what is now Ukraine, south of Russia, regularly killed mammoths—and built their houses out of neatly stacked mammoth bones. Picture a band of early American hunters spearing a terrified mammoth ambushed in a narrow streambed. Such hunts must have taken place many times.

Remember that the big mammals of the Americas had probably never seen humans before the Clovis hunters. Animals that evolved without humans around are surprisingly tame and unafraid. When I visited New Guinea's isolated Foja Mountains, which have no human population, I found the large tree kangaroos so tame that I could approach within a few yards of them. Probably the big mammals of the Americas were killed off before they could evolve a fear of humans.

Could Clovis hunters have killed mammoths fast enough to exterminate them? Modern elephants are slow breeders that take about twenty years to reproduce their numbers. Prehistoric mammoths probably bred slowly, too. Few other large animal species breed fast enough to reproduce their numbers in less than three years. It could have taken Clovis hunters only a few years to kill off the large mammals in a given area and then move on to the next area.

The Clovis hunters probably killed often, too. A mammoth might have 2,500 pounds of meat, but to use all that meat would mean preserving it by drying it. Would you go to the work of drying a ton of mammoth meat when you could just go kill another mammoth? Hunters probably used only part of the meat from each kill, along with other desirable parts such as skins and tusks.

We are all too familiar with the blitzkriegs by which modern European and American hunters nearly wiped out bison, whales, seals, and many other large animals. We also know that similar blitzkriegs occurred on oceanic islands when earlier hunters reached unoccupied lands. How could it have been different when the Clovis hunters entered an unoccupied New World?

CHAPTER 16

THE SECOND CLOUD

MY GENERATION IS THE FIRST IN HUMAN HISTORY to worry whether our children and grandchildren will survive, or will have a planet worth living on. That's because we as a species have two clouds hanging over us. These clouds could lead to similar results, but we view them very differently.

One cloud is the risk of a nuclear war that could destroy us all. That risk first revealed itself in the mushroom-shaped cloud over the Japanese city of Hiroshima, where the first atom bomb was dropped in 1945, during World War II. Everyone agrees that the nuclear risk is real. Nations have stockpiles of weapons, and politicians throughout history have occasionally made dumb mistakes. The nuclear risk shapes much of world diplomacy today.

(*left*)
Cattle graze where forest was recently cleared for pasture-land in the Amazon rain forest. Around the world, livestock grazing is a major contributor to deforestation and habitat loss.

The second cloud is the risk of an environmental collapse. One potential cause of such a collapse is the gradual extinction of most of the world's species. But while everyone agrees that a nuclear holocaust would be bad, there is great disagreement about whether the risk of a mass extinction is real—and about whether it would do much harm if it happened.

Is an Environmental Holocaust Under Way?
Figures from the International Council for Bird Preservation (ICBP) suggest that humans have caused about 1 percent of the world's bird species to go extinct within the last few centuries. What do people think about that?

At one extreme, many thoughtful people—especially economists and industrial leaders, but also some biologists and ordinary citizens—think that 1 percent is an overestimate and that the true loss has been smaller. But, they add, if it happened, losing 1 percent of bird species wouldn't matter.

At the opposite extreme, many other thoughtful people—especially conservation biologists and people who belong to environmental groups—think that 1 percent is an underestimate and that the true loss has been larger. They also think that mass extinction would greatly undermine the quality, or even the possibility, of human life. It will make a big difference to future generations which of these extreme views is closer to the truth.

How many species have humans driven into extinction? How many more are likely to go extinct in your lifetime, or your children's lifetimes? And what does it matter if they do? Aren't all species going to become extinct sometime or other? Is mass extinction a fantasy, a real risk for the future, or a crisis that's already well under way?

To answer these questions we first need realistic numbers. We need to find out how many species have gone extinct in modern times— that is, since 1600, when scientific naming and classification of species was just beginning. Then we need to estimate how many extinctions were caused by humans before 1600, and how many might happen in the future. At that point we can ask what difference it all makes to us anyway.

Modern Extinctions

Where did the figure of 1 percent of bird species lost since 1600 come from? The ICBP lists 108 species of bird, plus many additional subspecies, as having become extinct since 1600. Nearly all these extinctions were caused in some way by humans—more on that later in this chapter. Approximately 9,000 species of birds exist today. The 108 extinct species is almost 1 percent of 9,000.

But the ICBP calls a species extinct only after it has been specifically searched for in a place where it was once known to exist, or where it might turn up. What about birds that haven't been deliberately searched for? In Europe and North America, hundreds of thousands of fanatical birdwatchers monitor the status of bird species every year. Unfortunately, this does not apply to plants and animals. It doesn't even apply to birds in many parts of the world.

Most countries in the tropics, where the overwhelming majority of species live, have few birdwatchers. The status of many tropical species is unknown because no one has seen them or specifically looked for them since they were discovered. One example from New Guinea is Brass's friarbird. It is known only from eighteen specimens found at a single lagoon in 1939. No scientist has gone back to that lagoon, so we know nothing about the status of Brass's Friarbird today.

At least we know where to look for that friarbird. Many other species are known from collections made by nineteenth-century explorers. Sometimes they gave vague information about where they collected the birds. Try settling the status of a species when you have only "South America" to tell you where to look! So one problem in answering questions about extinction is that we do not know whether or not many named species still exist. But could species have gone extinct before they were even named?

Of course they could. Scientists think the total number of the world's species is around thirty million, but fewer than two million have been identified and named. An example from the plant world shows why we can be sure that many species vanished before being named. Botanist Alwyn Gentry surveyed the plants of Centinela, an isolated ridge in the South American nation of Ecuador. He found thirty-eight new plant species that grew on that ridge and nowhere else. Soon afterward, the ridge was logged and those plants were exterminated.

It was pure accident that Gentry visited Centinela before it was logged. Thousands of species of plants, snails, and other creatures must have existed on countless other ridges now cleared. We exterminated those species before we even discovered them.

MALAYSIA'S MISSING FISH

TROPICAL COUNTRIES TEND TO BE RICH IN SPECIES. But between growing populations and economic demands, many of them face pressure on their environments and resources. The Southeast Asian nation of Malaysia is typical. The case of its missing fish shows how this pressure can lead to extinction. Biological explorers had identified 266 species of fish in the forest rivers of Malaysia. But after most of the country's lowland forest was cut down, a search that lasted four years was able to find only 122 of those species—fewer than half. The other 144 Malaysian freshwater fish species must either be very rare and limited to small areas, or extinct. They reached that status before anyone noticed it. If Malaysia has already or almost lost half its freshwater fish species, this gives us a reasonable ballpark figure for the status of plants, fish, and many other kinds of species elsewhere in the tropics.

A cyprinid, native to Malaysia.

Past Extinctions

We know that species have become extinct since 1600 because the world's human population has grown in numbers, moved into uninhabited areas, and invented increasingly destructive technologies. What about human-caused extinctions before 1600? Is there a way to estimate them?

Fifty thousand years ago our species was confined to Africa and the warmer parts of Europe and Asia. Between then and 1600, we expanded to occupy the other continents and most oceanic islands. We also underwent a massive expansion in numbers, from perhaps a few million people fifty thousand years ago to about half a billion in 1600. We've already seen in chapters 14 and 15 that in every part of the world paleontologists have studied, and where humans arrived within the last fifty thousand years, waves of extinctions happened around the same time the humans arrived.

Ever since scientists realized this, they've argued over whether humans caused the extinctions or just happened to arrive at a bad time, when species were dying out because of changes in climate. There is no reasonable doubt that human activities caused the wave of bird extinctions on Polynesian islands and on Madagascar. As for earlier extinctions, especially those in Australia and the Americas, the cause is still being debated. But I doubt that climate did it. Climate swings did occur, but they did not cause waves of extinction every time they occurred, or everywhere they occurred. The extinction waves match up more closely with human arrival than with climate change.

Prehistoric people probably exterminated species not just in newly colonized lands but also in places where they had lived for a long time. Within the past twenty thousand years, Eurasia lost its mammoths, giant deer, and woolly rhinos. Africa lost its giant buffalo and giant horse. These big beasts may have been wiped out by humans who had been hunting them for a long time and who suddenly developed better weapons than ever before. The big animals disappeared for the same reasons that California's grizzly bears and Britain's bears, wolves, and beavers disappeared in modern times, after being hunted for thousands of years. Those reasons were more people and better weapons.

No one has ever tried to guess how many plant, lizard, or insect species were exterminated by prehistoric humans. Studies of bird extinction on islands, though, suggest that prehistoric humans on islands killed off about two thousand species—a fifth of all the bird species that existed a few thousand years ago. That doesn't count bird species that may have been exterminated on *continents* in prehistoric times. As for large mammals, scientists have looked at the disappearance not just of species but of genera, which are groups of related species. In North America, 73 percent of the genera of large mammals became extinct at the time humans arrived or afterward. For South America and Australia, the figures are 80 and 86 percent.

Future Extinctions

Is the peak of the human-caused extinction wave already past, or is most still to come? There are a couple of ways to think about this question.

One way to predict future extinctions is to think that tomorrow's extinct species will come from the list of species that are endangered today. How many species that still exist have had their numbers reduced to dangerously low levels? The International Council for Bird Preservation estimates that at least 1,666 bird species are either endangered or at risk of becoming extinct soon. That's almost 20 percent, or one-fifth, of the world's surviving birds. I said "at least 1,666" because this number is a low estimate. It is based just on species whose status caught scientists' attention, not on a survey of the status of all bird species.

Birds are not the only species at risk, of course. Numerous species of mammals, fish, reptiles and amphibians, insects and other small creatures, and plants are also known to be on the brink of extinction.

Another way to think about future extinctions is to understand the ways we exterminate species. Our growing population drives species to extinction in four main ways: overhunting, species introduction, habitat destruction, and ripple effects. Let's see if any of these has leveled off.

Overhunting means killing animals faster than they can maintain their numbers by breeding. It's the main way we've exterminated big animals. Have we already killed off all the big animals we might kill off? No. After overhunting drove down the number of whales, most countries signed an international ban on hunting whales for commercial purposes. Japan, however, tripled the number of whales it allowed to be killed for "scientific reasons." Africa's rhinos and elephants are being slaughtered at an increasing rate for their horns and ivory. At these rates, not just rhinos and elephants but most other large mammals of Southeast Asia and Africa—that is, those outside zoos and game parks—will be extinct within a few decades.

Species introduction means introducing species to parts of the world, either accidentally or on purpose, where they didn't previously live. In the United States, for example, the introduced species that are now firmly established include Norway rats, European starlings, and the fungi that are damaging our Dutch elm and chestnut trees. None of these or other introduced species is native to North America. All were brought there, accidentally or on purpose, by humans.

When species are introduced to a new area, they often exterminate some native species, either by eating them or by causing diseases. New Zealand bird species that nest on the ground, for example, are threatened by non-native rats that eat eggs and young birds.

American chestnut trees are another example. They have been practically exterminated by chestnut blight, an Asian fungus. That fungus doesn't harm chestnut trees in Asia because they had time to evolve defenses against it.

We are still spreading pests around the world, although many islands remain free of goats and Norway rats, and countries try to keep insects and diseases from entering. Good intentions do not guarantee good outcomes. What might be the biggest extinction wave in modern times was started a few decades ago in Africa's Lake Victoria, home to hundreds of fish species found nowhere else. People deliberately introduced a large fish called the Nile perch to the lake, thinking it would make a good commercial food source. The Nile perch is a predator that is now eating its way through Lake Victoria's unique species.

Habitat destruction is the third way we exterminate species. Most species live in a particular type of habitat and that habitat only. Marsh warblers are bird that live in marshes, while pine warblers live in pine forests. When the marshes are drained or the forests cut, the species that depend on those habitats are eliminated. Cebu Island in the Philippines once had ten species of birds that lived only on that island. When all the forest on Cebu Island was logged, nine of those species became extinct.

The worst habitat destruction is still to come. We are beginning to destroy the world's tropical rain forests, which cover only 6 percent of the earth's surface but are home to more than half its species. Brazil's Atlantic forest and Malaysia's lowland forest are almost completely gone, and those of Borneo and the Philippines are going. By the middle of the twenty-first century, the only large tracts of tropical rain forest likely to be surviving will be in parts of the Amazon Basin of South America and the Democratic Republic of Congo in Africa.

The ripple effect, the fourth form of habitat destruction, occurs when an action has unexpected results. Every species depends on other species for food and habitat. Species are connected to one another like branching rows of dominoes. Toppling one domino causes others to fall. Removing one species may lead to the loss of others, which in turn can push still other species to the brink.

THE JAGUAR AND THE ANTBIRD

NATURE CONSISTS OF SO MANY SPECIES,
connected to one another in such complex ways,
that it's impossible to foresee where the ripple
effects from the loss of one species may lead. The
fate of the little antbird on Barro Colorado Island
in Panama shows the ripple effect in action.

In the middle of the twentieth century, Barro
Colorado had three big predators: jaguars,
pumas, and harpy eagles. No one expected that
the removal of those predators would lead to the
extinction on the island of the little antbird, and to
massive changes in the island's forests. But it did.

The three big predators used to eat medium-
size predators, such as monkeys, peccaries (a
type of wild pig), and coatimundis (a relative of
raccoons). The big predators also ate medium-
size seed eaters, such as agoutis and pacas (two
types of rodents). With the disappearance of the
big predators, there was a population explosion

of the medium-size predators, who gobbled up the antbirds and their eggs. There was also an explosion of medium-size seed eaters, who ate large seeds that had fallen on the ground. This made it harder for trees with large seeds to replace themselves and spread, and easier for trees with small seeds to do so.

As the forests of Barro Colorado shift toward having more of the small-seeded trees and fewer large-seeded ones, other changes will occur. Species that feed on small seeds, such as mice and rats, will have their own population explosion, and this in turn will lead to greater numbers of the hawks, owls, and ocelots (small jungle cats) that feed on mice and rats.

Jaguars, pumas, and harpy eagles were never common on Barro Colorado. But their complete removal from the island had a ripple effect on the whole plant and animal community, including the extinction of many other species.

Barro Colorado Island.

Why Does Extinction Matter?

Isn't extinction a natural process? If so, why should we worry about the extinctions that are happening now?

Yes, every species will eventually go extinct. But the current human-caused rate of extinction is much higher than the natural rate. We know from the fossil record the average rate at which species became extinct over long periods of geological time. For birds, for example, the natural extinction rate averages less than one species each century. Today, though, we are losing at least two bird species each *year*—two hundred times the natural extinction rate. Not worrying about today's extinction wave because extinction is natural would be like not worrying about mass murder because death is the natural fate of all humans.

As to why we should worry about mass extinction, remember the ripple effect. The species we depend on depend on other species. Can you say which ten tree species produce most of the world's paper? For each of those ten trees, which are the ten bird species that eat most of the tree's insect pests, the ten insect species that pollinate most of its flowers, and the ten animal species that spread most of its seeds? Which species do those birds, insects, and animals depend on? You'd have to be able to answer those questions if you were the president of a timber company trying to figure out which species you could afford to let go extinct.

Compare the two clouds I mentioned at the beginning of this chapter, the ones hanging over our future. A nuclear holocaust is certain to be a disaster for us, but it isn't happening now, and it may never happen. An environmental holocaust is equally certain to be a disaster, but it is already well under way. It started tens of thousands of years ago and it is currently causing more damage than ever before—and the rate of destruction is increasing. Will we now choose to stop it?

NOTHING LEARNED,
EVERYTHING FORGOTTEN?

THE THEMES OF THIS BOOK COME TOGETHER IN our rise over the past three million years—and also in the way we now stand on the verge of reversing all our progress.

The first signs that our ancestors were unusual among animals were the crude stone tools that appeared in Africa 2.5 million years ago. Although tools were becoming a regular, important part of our livelihood, they did not trigger a big jump in our development as a species.

For another 1.5 million years we remained in Africa. Around a million years ago we spread to the warm areas of Europe and Asia. This

(left)
Barro Colorado Island.

made us the most widespread of the three chimpanzee species—but still much less widespread than lions. By 100,000 years ago, at least, Neanderthal humans were using fire, but in other ways we were still just another big mammal. We had not developed a trace of art, architecture, or high technology. No one knows whether we had developed language, drug addictions, or our mating habits and life cycle.

Clear evidence of a Great Leap Forward shows up suddenly in Europe about sixty thousand years ago, at the same time that anatomically modern humans, *Homo sapiens*, arrived from Africa. Art appeared, along with technology based on specialized tools for various uses. Human cultures began showing differences across time and place. Whatever caused this leap, it must have used only a tiny fraction of our genes. We still differ from chimps in just 1.6 percent of our genetic makeup, and most of that difference formed before our Great Leap in behavior. My best guess is that the Leap was triggered when we became capable of language.

These first modern humans bore noble traits, but they also bore two traits that lie at the root of our modern problems. One is our tendency to murder each other in large numbers. The other is our tendency to destroy our environment and our resource base. If the seeds of self-destruction have been closely linked to the rise of advanced civilizations in other solar systems as well, it is easy to understand why we have not been visited by any flying saucers.

At the end of the last Ice Age, ten thousand years ago, the rise of our civilization gained speed. We occupied the Americas—at the same time that many large mammals disappeared from those continents. Soon agriculture began. A few thousand years later, the first written texts appeared. Our early writings record our progress and inventiveness, but they also show that addiction and genocide were already part of human life. Habitat destruction started to undermine many societies. The first human settlers in Polynesia and Madagascar caused mass exterminations of species. Histories written since that time have traced our rise and fall in detail.

Since the 1940s we have had the means to blow ourselves up overnight. Even if we don't blunder into that quick end, starvation, pollution, and destructive technology are increasing. Farmland, food stocks in the sea, and other natural resources are decreasing. So is the environment's ability to absorb wastes. As more people with more power scramble for fewer resources, something has to give.

What is likely to happen?

There are many reasons to fear the worst. Even if all humans vanished tomorrow, our environment is so damaged that it would keep degrading for decades. Too many species to count already belong to the "living dead"—individuals remain, but their numbers are too few to keep the population going.

Despite what we could have learned from our past self-destructive behavior, many people who should know better think there is no reason to limit our population numbers or to stop assaulting our environment. Some join that assault for profit or out of ignorance. Many more are desperate to survive, and don't have the luxury of thinking about the future. All these facts suggest that destruction is unstoppable and that we humans, too, are among the living dead, with a future as bleak as that of the other two chimpanzees.

This grim view is captured in a sentence written in 1912 by Arthur Wichmann, a Dutch

explorer and professor. Seeing explorers in
New Guinea make the same mistakes over and
over again, leading to unnecessary suffering
and death, Wichmann predicted that future
explorers would continue to make the same
mistakes. "Nothing learned," he wrote, "and
everything forgotten!"

But I believe our situation is *not* hopeless.
We are the only ones creating our problems, so
it's completely within our power to solve them.
We are the only animals that can learn from the
experiences of other members of our species living
in distant places or in the past. Among the hopeful
signs are many realistic ways to avoid disaster,
such as by limiting human population growth,
preserving natural habitats, and adopting other
environmental safeguards. Many governments are
already doing some of these things.

Awareness of environmental problems is
spreading. Many countries have lowered their
rate of population growth. Genocide has not
vanished, but the spread of communication
technology may reduce our xenophobia, making
it harder to see distant people as subhuman or
different from us. I was seven years old when
the A-bombs were dropped on Hiroshima and

Nagasaki in 1945. I remember that for decades afterward, people felt that nuclear destruction could happen at any moment. But that risk now seems more remote than at any time since those bombs fell. These are reasons for hope.

We don't need new, still-to-be-invented technology to solve our problems. We just need more governments to do many more of the same things that some are already doing. And the average citizen is not powerless. In recent years, citizen groups have helped fight the extinction of many species. Commercial whaling and the hunting of big cats for fur coats are just two examples of harmful activities that have been greatly reduced because of changes in the public's attitudes.

I see us facing serious problems and an uncertain future, but I am cautiously hopeful. Even Wichmann's grim prediction turned out to be false. Explorers in New Guinea since his time *have* learned from the past and avoided the disasters of those who went before.

A better motto for our future may come from Otto von Bismarck, a German statesman who worked in European politics for decades. Even though he had seen many errors and much stupidity, Bismarck still believed it was possible to learn from history. He wrote about his life and dedicated the work "to [my] children and grandchildren, towards an understanding of the past, and for guidance for the future."

This is the spirit in which I dedicate this book to my young sons and their generation. If we learn from the past that I have traced, our future may be brighter than that of the other two chimpanzees.

Glossary

anatomy the study of the structure of organisms, or the inner and outer shapes of plants and animals

anthropology the study of human beings; various branches of anthropology focus on human origins, on the biological and social features of human populations, on the relationships of people with their environments and with other groups of people, on family structures, and on the differences and similarities among cultures

archaeology the study of past human cultures through their physical remains, such as fossils, skeletons, buildings, and objects they made and used

artifact something made by humans, such as a tool, a household utensil, or a piece of clothing or jewelry

biogeography the study of how the different species of plants and animals are distributed, or spread, across the earth's surface

colonize to settle in a new territory and establish political control over it

Cro-Magnon a member of an early population of humans first identified from forty-thousand-year-old skeletons found in a cave called Cro-Magnon in southern France; they were modern humans belonging to the same species as people today, *Homo sapiens*

DNA short for deoxyribonucleic acid; the set of molecules that contain the genetic code for each living thing, and that are the basis for genetic traits passed from parents to their offspring; DNA is made up of genes grouped into strands called chromosomes

ecology the study of the connections and relationships among living things and their environments

ethical having to do with ethics or morality, which is the consideration of what is good and bad, or right and wrong, behavior

Eurasia the large land mass that contains the continents of Europe and Asia

evolution the changing pattern of life forms over time as new species arise because of mutations, and old species become extinct

exterminate to destroy, kill off, or wipe out something, usually by a deliberate effort

extinct died out, no longer in existence

first contact to anthropologists, the first meeting between two peoples or cultures when one is more technologically advanced than the other; first contacts usually lead to dramatic changes in the less advanced culture's way of life

fossil something from a past time in earth's history that has been preserved by being turned to stone; bones, plants, and footprints are among the traces of ancient life that have survived as fossils

gene a distinct series or sequence of nucleic acids, part of the genetic code carried in DNA

genetics the branch of biology that studies the ways DNA causes variety and heredity in living things

genocide a deliberate, often organized, attempt to destroy a particular group; populations have been targeted for genocide because of their race, religion, national or ethnic origin, or for other reasons

heredity in genetics, the passing of features and traits from parents to offspring; traits passed on in this way are called inherited traits

hunter-gatherers people who follow a lifestyle called hunting and gathering, which means living by hunting game animals and gathering wild food plants; for most of human history, everyone was a hunter-gatherer, and a few small groups still are

lineage the line of descent from an ancestor; every organism whose origins can be traced to the same shared ancestor belongs to one lineage

mammal a member of the class of warm-blooded animals that have a backbone, nurse their young from the mother's mammary glands, and usually have some hair on their skins

millennium a thousand years

molecular biology the branch of biology that studies the chemical makeup of living organisms and their cells, with special interest in the molecules that create proteins in organisms and those involved in heredity

mutation in genetics, a change in the structure
of a gene or chromosome that leads to an
organism having traits or features that its
parents did not have; a mutation may have
no noticeable effect, or it may be harmful
to the organism, or it may be favorable and
improve the organism's chances of survival;
evolution is a drive by favorable mutations
that leads to the development of new species

Neanderthal a member of an early population
of humans first identified in skeletons
from the Neander Valley in Germany;
Neanderthals were a different species than
modern humans

paleobotany the study of fossil plants or of plant
life in earlier eras

paleontology the study of life in past eras of
earth's history, mostly based on fossils

paleopathology the study of ancient diseases and
physical ailments

physiology the study of how biological
structures, such as blood, skeletons, and
internal organs, work

polygamy type of marriage in which a spouse
can be married to multiple partners at the
same time

polygyny type of polygamy in which a man can be married to more than one woman

primate a member of the group of mammals that includes humans, apes, monkeys, and various small animals such as lemurs, tarsiers, and bush babies; primates have hands and sometimes feet that are well developed for handling and picking up objects, with opposable thumbs and sometimes opposable big toes; most primates have flat nails, not claws, on their hands and feet

protohuman having to do with an early form of humans or with the ancestors of humans

syntax the part of grammar that has to do with the way words are joined together to create meaningful phrases or sentences; different languages may have different syntaxes, as shown in word order—for example, some languages put verbs at the ends of sentences

toxic poisonous or damaging

xenophobia fear and dislike or hatred of those who are different or foreign

zoology the branch of biology that studies animal life

Index

About the Authors

JARED DIAMOND is professor of geography at the University of California, Lost Angeles. He has published over 200 articles in *Discover, Natural History, Nature*, and *Geo* magazines. His is the author of several books including *Guns, Germs, and Steel,* which was awarded the Pulitzer Prize and has sold over 1.5 million copies, the international bestseller *Collapse,* and the recently published *The World Until Yesterday: What Can We Learn from Traditional Societies?*

REBECCA STEFOFF is the author of a biography of the Shawnee chieftan Tecumseh and a ten-volume series of historical atlases, among many other books for children and young adults. She has adapted Howard Zinn's celebrated *A Young People's History of the United States* and Ronald Takaki's *A Different Mirror for Young People.* She lives in Portland, Oregon.